RELATIONSHIPS: GIFTS OF THE SPIRIT

I relate to very Chapter 5. good information.

RELATIONSHIPS: GIFTS OF THE SPIRIT

How to view challenging relationships as
opportunities for growth

Julie Hutslar

Luminous Epinoia Press
Cedar City

Luminous Epinoia Press
PO 1224 Cedar City, UT 84721
Copyright © 2004 by Julie Hutslar

Printed in the United States of America

ISBN: 0-9753000-4-0

Library of Congress Control Number: 2004092158

Printed on acid free paper

Cover and inside artwork copyright © 2004 by Julie Hutslar
Artist's and author's website: www.jrhutslar.com

Publisher's website: www.luminousepinoia.com

*To my greatest challenge and also my greatest support,
my husband and best friend.*

Foreword

Every experience we have leaves its mark, or change, on and in us. None of us are as flexible and mobile at eighty years old as we were at eight. That means flexible in body as well as in mind or attitude. Certainly one of the effects of the act of living life is to help form our beliefs about exactly what is this life we are living, or, to some, being forced to live. Our beliefs in turn affect the very life that has, and still is helping form those same beliefs. We are caught in a loop wherein everything we do or think influences everything we do or think.

My beliefs have been formed by that same cycle of events, but are different than your beliefs because my life has not been yours. Specifically my beliefs have been formed, in part, by the pain and suffering I have been privileged to feel and witness. Now that may seem like a strange word to use, *privileged,* but the work I do has hinged on those two extremely prevalent human experiences, pain and suffering. My speciality is in working with people who suffer from chronic pain. Chronic pain is different than acute pain in that it is somewhere between difficult and impossible to pinpoint its exact source. Acute pain is simple; you stub your toe, then your toe hurts. Chronic pain permeates your entire life; your sleep, your appetite, your attitude, and your emotional being itself. Chronic pain robs you of the very life you thought you were born to live. Chronic pain also helps establish those belief patterns that, in turn, form the life that establishes your belief patterns.

It sometimes feels that life is no more than a ride on a cruel merry-go-round. Is there really no way off? Are we doomed to live as pawns, some with lives more fortunate than others, but still only subject to a seemingly random deposition of good or bad luck? Is one day only to be followed by another, replete with its own set of hidden challenges? Or, as Julie Hutslar presents in this book, can we be co-creators of our own existences, actually choreographing the dance that is our very lives?

The experience with my patients has changed my belief patterns over the past twenty years. In the beginning of my career working with the human body, I believed that we got old, we hurt more, we wore out, then we died. Now, twenty plus years later, the only thing I believe is that we get older then we die at some point, but the path we take is neither predetermined, nor is it out of our own control. There is rarely a day in my work where at least one person, of varying ages, tells me that they are just getting old and wearing out, believing that to be the source of their pains. I can counter that statement with hundreds of others who are both older, and in less pain. Wherein lies the difference? The answer is clear. It is in their belief patterns.

The patients I work with who have retained a positive, flexible, mobile, and open attitude about life and its effects upon them have less pain and a more enjoyable quality of life than do those who are victims of their own lives. I don't only mean the intangible pains of life either. I mean the actual presentation of physical pain and suffering.

Now if that idea resonates as true, or maybe just possible to you, then you may want to learn how to apply that to your own life. The steps are quite simple, but the execution of the steps must become integral to one's own life journey.

Ms. Hutslar presents a different view of life in this book. By different, I mean a way of looking at things out of eyes that see a much bigger picture than the eyes that only see the suffering of daily living. She has isolated the *relationships* portion of life, but I think her views on how to see relationships can be applied to all things with immeasurable benefit. Rather than live life as a victim, she tells how we can see everything that happens to us as our very own soul's gift. Our lives then become a blessing and a fortune rather than a torture that will only end with a blessed death. In my work I suggest to my patients that the pain they feel is always their body's (or even the deeper parts of themselves) way to send them (their cognizant mind) a message. An example of acute pain would be an intense pain in your hand that is saying, "Get your hand off the stove!" An example of chronic pain that has immobilized you through lower back spasm might be saying, "I'm terrified because I think I'm about to lose my job and I won't be able to make the mortgage payment and my entire life is falling out from under me." Or it might have just said, "We're too old to lift ten 80-pound bags of cement out of the truck." Either way, your body gave you a message. If you heed the message, the quality of your life will unquestionably improve. If you don't, the message will be repeated, oftentimes at an increased level of severity.

In this book Julie gives many examples of how a relationship (no matter how tormenting it may seem) can be seen as a message and a learning and growing experience. Just as in heeding the messages of the body, learning from our relationships can unquestionably improve the quality of our lives. Read ahead and learn how.

I believe that Julie Hutslar's perspective on the events, relationships, and traumas of our lives can improve the quality of our lives, and thus change the belief patterns that affect the lives that in turn create the belief patterns...

None of us can prevent the death of our physical bodies, but all of us can learn ways to make the journey a more spiritually fulfilling one. Happy reading, you won't be the same when you've finished this book.

Dr. Edward Hunt
Pinnacle Health Center
Specializing in the treatment of chronic pain

In Appreciation

There are many authors who either directly or indirectly influenced my thinking and thus, this book. I feel they are positively effecting change in a world that has been long awaiting it. They are those that assist others in their own spiritual quests, through their words and actions. I would like to thank and acknowledge the following as I directly refer to their works in this book.

Carolyn Myss has been a voice in my mind since I read her very first book and would greatly encourage anyone who is searching to find time with all her books, but especially *Anatomy of the Spirit* and *Sacred Contracts*. Gary Zukov with the *Seat of the Soul*, James Hillman and *The Soul's Code*, Michael Moore and his documentary *Bowling for Columbine*, Barry Glassner's *The Culture of Fear* offer great insights and inspire equally great questions. A special thanks to Ani DiFranco, forever a creative inspiration, for her words quoted from *Reckoning/Revelling*.

Thanks to those who participated and wrote the *Findhorn Experience*, thus inspiring non-physical communication with Nature. Also, my brain did somersaults many times while reading

Michael Road's *Journey into Oneness* and I would not hesitate to recommend all his books. And that goes for Elaine Pagels as well with *Origins of Satan, Gnostic Gospels,* and *Beyond Belief.* Yehuda Berg with the *72 Names of God*, Richard Bach's *Illusions*, and J. K. Rowling's *Harry Potter* series all entertained and inspired the impossible to come into the realm of the possible.

Thanks to those television and motion picture shows that brought my subtle body characters: *Startrek, Beverly Hillbillies,* and *Species* as well as *The Kid* and *Thomasina.* Appreciation to Lincoln Barnett for his lovely text *The Universe and Dr. Einstein* and Thubten Chodron's *Open Heart, Clear Mind.*

A very special thanks to Bonnie Wehle for being such a thorough and stimulating editor, my sister Jan for *The Gift*, Gabrell Carroll for his ingenious healing techniques (you can contact him at *livingvision@earthlink.net*), George Conley for assisting in reconnecting me to the Divine, Maggie Wood for being the original inspiration for this book, and to my family for their unwitting participation in my relationships research. Many others have influenced my work and my spiritual process; a healthy thank you is the least I can do. Each relationship, in its own way, has assisted me with uncovering my own spiritual contracts, fulfilling those contracts is what I now can give back.

GIFTS OF THE SPIRIT

Contents

Good

101

1 Purpose of Relationships

Inertia: a property of matter whereby it remains at rest or continues in uniform motion unless acted upon by some outside force.

Inertia resists change, says Newton, and according to him, constitutes a fundamental principal of the universe. I believe that the same law influences our choice of relationships. In the human struggle to survive over the millennia, we have found that fiercely clinging to what we have has provided the security necessary for survival. This may have its physical merits, however, for the soul to progress on its evolutionary path, it must grow and *change*. In order for change to occur, and the necessary growth that awaits, we need a force to come along and encourage us in one direction or another. Our distinctly *human* nature tries to keep us in the uniform motion that we so much want to believe will keep us secure. This is where relationships come in. I believe that all relationships exist for a reason, consciously planned or not. We are tossed together by physical proximity or by blood. Each of us are in each others lives for the express purpose of being challenged and hopefully growing in ways that we wouldn't without this out-side force acting upon us. We are a life continuing in uniform motion (inertia). A relationship and its subsequent reactions are the outside forces creating change. *Each relationship, no matter how challenging, is truly a spiritual gift created by the individuals involved to act as a catalyst for growth.*

That being said, if we look at all relationships through this somewhat different set of lenses, how would that affect all our present and future relationships? If we could see each conflictual interaction or challenging partner as a ploy for healing and growth, wouldn't that change the nature of each encounter with them? Wouldn't that change the nature of the relationship itself? And what if we devote more of our energy and efforts to understand-ing relationships and seeing them for the gifts that they are? We could reap the benefits of our soul's own spiritual evolution and also avoid the never-ending cycle of repeating the same relation-ship patterns again and again until we finally, in utter exhaustion, grasp our lesson.

Do you find yourself dating the same personality type, even though they have the same detrimental effects to your well-be-ing? Did you marry someone just like your mother? Are you watch-ing your son develop attributes uncommonly similar to your father's? Quite often you can see the same traits repeated in your in-laws, your bosses, your coworkers or teenagers. When more than one person in your life elicits the same emotional response from you, there is an issue at hand. There is most likely a pattern presenting itself and an opportunity to discover something about *you.* I believe your unconscious decision maker (whether you call it your soul, your fate, or your unconscious) has carefully chosen certain individuals with traits that challenge in order to move you on to a different, hopefully more evolved way of looking at things.

The reason I believe we choose relationships to work out soul-ful issues is because we humans are, for the most part, naturally social creatures. We are born of other humans and exist with other humans and need and desire other humans for companionship, acceptance, or for whatever they may bring. I don't really see an easy way to avoid relationships in this human incarnation. So, since we are stuck with them, and many of them are so intense, my goal is to offer some creative wisdom and unique ideas for coping, understanding, and finding joy and fulfillment in even the most challenging relationships.

CREATED REALITIES

The reality you see around you may not be the reality I see around me. For example, once I was sitting at the local airport watching the evening sky accumulate dark clouds. I was enjoying the colors of the late sun on the bottoms of the thick clouds, and how they were shaping the sunset. I saw them as an inspiration for a painting. The man I was speaking with was a flight instructor and saw the clouds for their meteorological meaning and what that would mean for late-afternoon students. Another pilot wanted to return north to his home and saw them as negative factors to his safe trip, flying his small aircraft back to the family that he missed. They could even be life threatening. Another individual at the airport saw the potential for rain in those clouds that was so desperately needed by his crops. Still another saw the same clouds as an opportunity to practice her newly acquired skill of instrument flying, flying in the clouds. Some other people may have looked at the clouds and not registered a thing; some may have reflected on their beauty, some may have felt concern for the safety of the individuals in the back of the commuter plane who were their responsibility, and so on. You can see how the very same meteorological condition could create different emotional responses in many people's unique worlds. That is not to say that the world actually manifests itself differently for one person than another. Our response to what the world presents is in accord with our own personal universe. Those places, cultures and climates where we find ourselves are also a part of the universe we have co-created. The beliefs we carry personally color our own unique world.

Let me give you another example. If you have a belief that the world is limited, limited in resources as well as opportunities; if you believe that there are only a certain number of great jobs, or only so much wealth, or so many natural resources, then you will find yourself upholding that reality. How? You will find scarcity in your own life: scarcity of funds, of resources, difficulty in accepting others who use fossil fuels carelessly, and difficulty in believing you should have abundance in such a limited world. The converse of that is the belief that the universe is limitless, boundless in resources. Even after the earth's fossil fuels are depleted there will be many more resources to supply us with our needs while in this incarnation. This view of reality sees people receiving bountiful blessings. Why, because they deserve them? No, deserving has nothing to do with it and is based on judgment anyway. Their reality is dictated by their own beliefs. If they want to squander resources and money or whatever else they feel like, those in the scarcity mentality may suffer, but those in the bountiful won't feel a twinge of guilt. Their belief is so firm that their universe upholds it, and they have no evidence of otherwise. We have all known people living both these scenarios. The bountiful ones are like King Midas, everything they touch turns to gold. The others are usually conscientious, socially active, considerate people, but often struggle financially. Life doesn't seem fair, does it? Not from this viewpoint, no. Let's explore these core beliefs some more and how relationships enter as a catalyst for removing or changing these beliefs for, as we have illustrated, some can be quite limiting without our cognitive awareness.

ENERGY AS POWER

My personal source of guidance in these matters (well, aside from lifetimes of relationships myself, learning the hard way) is through my experiences as an energy worker. Not on the payroll for the utility company, I do work in human power nevertheless. I work to locate the energetic source of negative beliefs or images about oneself or the world that is in any way restrictive. Where we allocate energy is where we place our power. In my healing sessions, I have realized many things about humans, but the most outstanding is that we need assistance and understanding in relationships. Part of what I do is recreate a previously experienced moment in time and locate the vibrations, or emotions, affecting each participant. The one thing that is always glaringly obvious is that each individual thinks the others are thinking something entirely different than they actually are, and then base decisions about themselves on those incorrect assumptions. Like in those romantic comedy movies where the viewer sees the whole story, but the would-be lover only sees glimpses at the most inopportune time and gets bizarre ideas about the innocent protagonist. For example, Tim may live his whole life thinking his father does not love him. He tries to gain his acceptance and love, but it appears to Tim that nothing he does or says gains any amount of special attention from his father. Looking at Tim's father, we see a man emotionally shut down who was raised in a society that taught him never to get mushy or to express outward feelings of love. He truly admires Tim, but doesn't want to bring him up the same way he was brought up, so he chooses to exclude him from his *traditionally male* world. Still, Tim's father does not have the communication skills to express externally what he feels about Tim internally, leaving Tim feeling cut off and making assumptions about his father's lack of feelings towards him. Keep in mind, parents are just people who are a little bit older than us and are not perfect. Tim's father feels the unspoken disdain of his own way of life from Tim, since they are so completely different. If they never communicate these things, and in most relationships I find we operate from unspoken assumptions, they are both experiencing life and basing realities on untruths. They are living out dramas that could be rectified, challenges that could be solved which could reap benefits long before Tim's father seeks clarity on his deathbed.

So my purpose for this book is twofold. First, I want to present many of the variables that keep us from understanding one another. Second, I hope to present ways to identify what we are potentially healing as we encounter our most challenging relationships. What does our soul want to learn through these interactions? Along the way, I hope to entertain, introduce interesting awarenesses and suggest some creative ideas on relationships that may brighten the human experience, bring joy and ultimately more genuine fulfillment.

EVERY RELATIONSHIP HAS A PURPOSE

To begin, I want to offer an assumption that you don't have to buy, but you have to entertain to follow along with this writing. That is that every relationship has a purpose. That includes those with your parents, your children, your lover/husband/wife/ significant other, coworkers, siblings and even neighbors. I would even go so far as to say that we *choose* these relationships, maybe even before we have moved to the town where we will then meet that someone. Our unconscious selves are working out the details of our soulful journey, and that does not mean just the mere 100 or so years you may live in the body you are now occupying. It means the journey of your soul, however long that has been, and wherever that has taken you. I am not here to analyze the details of the entire journey, only the *traveling together* part. I am suggesting that as incarnate beings (souls inhabiting a physical body) we are working through some things we have previously set in motion. Whether or not you believe in karma (those things that help determine the now, what you reap, you sow, that sort of thing), or reincarnation (previous existences), you can still entertain the premises of this writing. You must at least imagine the idea that the soul exists and has existed for a very long time and was probably experiencing something before this incarnation. And contained in those experiences, wherever they occurred, were events that created causes that set into motion effects. If you just want to expand your mind, you can enjoy this for whatever you personally get out of it. I need to start from somewhere. That somewhere is that we really are on a journey, one from which unfortunately we can only see a small part of the road.

Imagine you are walking along a road. It is a straight road with no obvious places to stop along the way. You may very well walk straight until you are prompted to either stop or go in another direction, as in Newton's theory wherein an object will continue on the same course forever unless something external acts upon it. What could act upon you, or prompt you, or lure you, or stop you; the weather, a yummy treat, a threat ahead? Maybe. I am looking at the most common theme or force: someone else. That someone else who may appear seemingly by coincidence, I propose, is the exact person you were meant to meet just at that time in order to move you to some other road on your journey. Keep in mind Newton's Second Law of Inertia which states the *amount* of force necessary to move an object depends upon the mass of the body being moved. In our case, how stubbornly are we attached to our preconceived beliefs and ideas? In effect, the more stubbornly attached we are, the greater our mass, then the greater the force needed to move us to a new place. Or as Albert Einstein is quoted as saying, "Nothing changes until something moves."

That is the thesis of this text. *All relationships are present as a catalyst for soul growth.* There is also the idea that there may be some karma to be finished or worked out through any given relationship, but I see both of those as the same thing. If you are still carrying around a debt to the universe and need to repay it, that is a negative weight, and by unloading it, you lighten your load, travel at a higher vibration, and resonate closer to your highest self. I believe that moving closer to the highest self is to a great extent the soul's goal.

EQUALING OUT AN ENERGETIC DEBT

What I am speaking about when I say a *debt to the universe* is that I think there is only an energetic sense of justice that exists. We as humans have created a lot of complicated ideas about justice depending upon which side of it we happen to be on, and these ideas have to do with human judgment about the concepts of right and wrong. My sense is that the universe is quite neutral. That it is only energy. For example, in a human incarnation you take a life, an energy being that weighs, let's say, 100 energy units. At some point in your soul's existence you will have to give back 100 of your own energy units. Perhaps not all at once, but the debt is there and the universe keeps track, non-judgmentally, not perceiving right or wrong, only that there is an imbalance. So our debts don't exactly consist of those things others think we have done wrong or even that *we* think we have done wrong, but simply of the same quality of energy that was taken (or given) being given (or received) back. For example, if you were a factory owner during the Industrial Revolution with many workers in your employment whom you treated with disrespect and violence, even though it may have been politically correct at the time, you may have a great deal of energy units of disrespect and violence to receive at some point along your soul's journey. And at the same time each of the workers were balancing out their own justice being born into an environment which supported such a system.

Subscribing to this neutral energy concept definitely brings a different awareness about even the most unimportant relationships. Instead of thinking you are laden with an ill mother or burdened with a hyperactive, angry child, you hopefully can begin to look differently, inwardly, to your own self, wondering, what is it about this caretaking of my elderly mother that is so necessary for me along my path that I don't understand? Hopefully, together we can uncover new ways not only to understand those currently in our lives, but also to actively seek out our future teachers, prepared and ready as fertile students.

HIGHER FREQUENCIES

Let me explain what I mean by the higher vibration that I spoke of earlier. Everything resonates at some wavelength, either slower or faster. People are no exception. Depending upon the type and amount of negative emotions you carry (anger, self-hate, powerlessness, resentment, etc.) you will appear lower on an energy frequency scale or as a slow vibration. The higher you vibrate depends upon the types of emotions and responses you emit such as love, sympathy, compassion, generosity, or acceptance, which vibrate faster on the scale of measurable frequencies. If these emotions were to be measured, hate and anger would appear on the bottom of the vibrational scale, whereas love would register at the top, the highest of frequencies. So when I speak of improving relationships by raising your vibration, I mean just that, dumping lower frequencies you resonate with and moving to a higher ground from which you can grow your new garden in the soil of a higher vibration.

I often hear people talk about failed romantic relationships saying, "That relationship was obviously not meant to be," or "That was seriously stupid of me to get involved with that person." Given this different way of looking at relationships, we might be inclined to say, "That wasn't meant to last a lifetime, but it did what it was meant to do." Or maybe even, "I wasn't ready to look at that personal attribute yet, and will be seeing that relationship again, in another form some day."

SPIRITUAL VERSUS SOCIETAL RELATIONSHIPS

My brother recently got married and asked for my opinion about some vows that would be more meaningful than the ordinary 'til death do us part' business. I introduced him to the concept that many relationships continue long after the death of the physical self and that others are ready to be extinguished long before we even approach a close proximity to physical death. I suggested he look at his ceremony more as a ritual of vows shared with those he cared for most, not limiting the relationship to the present body and also not confining it to it either. If both souls got what they were coming for, so to speak, they should be graciously allowed to move on. Gary Zukov writes about similar concepts in his book *Seat of the Soul*, calling them spiritual relationships, instead of relationships based on economic decisions. Often our parents or grandparents were bonded in marriage because there were no other economic choices. Men were not typically trained in taking care of children or homes and women were not allowed or compensated for outside work.

Today we are in a different position, or most of us in the West are anyway, but still we hold on to this concept of marriage and feel guilt or obligation long after the soul has lost its purpose for the relationship. I am not talking about lust versus agape love. Agape is unselfish, unconditional love for another. When a couple commits themselves to each other based on the chemical high of what I call lust, and then that chemistry wears off after the coupling has transpired, that is what I call genetic and human, for the purposes of procreation and prolonging of the species. It is very natural, and not to say unnecessary or even without reasons of its own. But in the relationships I am speaking of the commitment is based on some mutual understandings. These may come from economic reasons, but most people I work with and know personally are looking for what everyone calls their *soulmate*. That person who would complement them, enhance them, challenge them, someone who would understand the needs of their soul, and also would connect wonderfully in a physical way as well! These are spiritual relationships and may have their roots in a time much earlier than in this present life.

Carolyn Myss, in her video tape series called *Energy Anatomy*, talks about the idea of the soulmate. In her experience, it is not the prince charming we often imagine bringing flowers and whispering sweet nothings in our ears. Rather, she suggests looking around and identifying the one person who has caused you the most grief in this life. That is your soulmate. This also is my experience with relationships. The very reason that person is in your life, and you in theirs is for growth in a way that you couldn't do alone. They are the *external* forces acting upon you to cause change. They are inertia breakers.

I am not just speaking about primary relationships; mates, lovers, significant others, spouses. I am talking about *all* relationships. However, I believe that the ones closest to us bring us the most challenges. Those are the ones we have previous agreements with or with whom we are working out something important. We cannot escape them as easily as we can the more casual relationships that pepper our lives. I used to think that if you had issues with your family, you should move away, far away, to the other side of the continent (as I did) and then you would never have to deal with them. Wrong. They just wait, and are still there for you, distance does not make them go away.

In the following pages I will present concepts and ideas that hopefully will bring greater joy and happiness as well as learning and gratitude to the realm of relationships.

2 Energetics of Relationships

Let's look at the collection of beliefs we acquire and identify as being who we believe we are. For example, if you feel that you are worthless, subconsciously, your world arranges itself to accommodate that belief. You meet people who treat you as worthless, find jobs where you are not truly valued, and at the core of you is someone who says, " I may as well be set out by the curb on garage sale day." Your plans and ideas don't inspire confidence when unconsciously you know they were created without value. They don't carry the stamp of authority or validity. It is as if others have something you don't, some right that you weren't given because you weren't good enough. Then on top of the belief that you are worthless, you build another belief that you are inadequate, and on top of that one that you are unwanted and if you are unwanted (who would want someone who is worthless and inadequate?) then you are most likely unloved. If no one wants me, how do I find someone to love me? Occasionally someone gets in, but that person usually also resonates with the same negative self-images as we do, and so our relationship is based on us comforting each other in our own worthlessness. Do you see the strange, yet very common, path to a pretty low self-esteem?

ON WHAT STATION DO YOU BROADCAST?

Let me explain it energetically. When you listen to the radio, you tune in to a particular station, one that plays your favorite music, has your favorite DJ or talk show host. When you listen to that station, or frequency over the airwaves, everyone else who likes the same features of that station hears that same programming also. The people who listen to different stations do not hear the music you hear, they're not familiar with the ads, or the featured musicians. For example, they may listen to classical music. Maybe they enjoy hearing about the history of each composer. While another music lover listens to his favorite country music station and knows all the words by heart of his favorite songs. This is what it is like to resonate with different vibrations. You can't relate to your friend who knows all the songs on the country music station if you haven't been tuning in to that station, and he can't understand where you've been living to not know them. Chances are, though, you will attract people who enjoy the same music as you do. You share those common elements of life. You may frequent the same concerts or shows, buy the same products or speak the same lingo. It is the same thing with the common vibrations that permeate all aspects of our lives.

Quite often I find couples who are dating or married tend to have similar core beliefs or traits. I was working with a couple some time ago who illustrated this. The first session with one spouse was very meaningful, but later as I worked with the other, I felt like I was repeating the exact session. This couple carried the very same vibrations of inferiority coupled with powerlessness. As with the radio frequency, we attract those who have the same energy frequency. What station are you broadcasting without being consciously aware? Like radio or television waves which can't be seen, but still carry vast amounts of information, vibrations or beliefs held energetically are more powerful and carry more programming than we know.

In truth, we are not, at the core of us, these negative vibrations, such as worthless or inferior, but many of us believe we are. Don't get me wrong, we don't just pick up negative images of ourselves, we collect lots of positive ones. I just don't see any reason to disturb those. We wear these self-images as if they were our clothing, and then attract others which match and make up the perfect outfit. Even though we might not feel comfortable wearing our negative-image clothing, we feel it fits us perfectly. Quite often you can identify friends who hang out together by their similar looking outfits, be they designer dresses or negative self-images. This is just another way to locate like-minded people.

ENERGY LIKE ELECTRICITY

The way I use the term energy is similar to how you would describe electricity. Energy is the life force of the thing it is animating. In our case, the thing being animated is us: people. In the case of electricity, it may be a lamp or a stereo or a stove. You cannot see electricity, but when you flip on the light switch, you witness its power. This is what it is like when you are plugged into a belief, either positive or negative. If you have put energy into the belief, it has power. That means it creates reality for you, just as the electricity acting through the light plugged into the wall produces light.

For example, if you believe at your core, and that is where these beliefs are held, at our very core, that you were never wanted as a child, that your parents didn't really want children or a child of your gender, or you specifically, you might resonate with the vibration of "unwanted." This vibration does not judge, it does not know if it is positive or negative, but simply that it is part of who you are. This vibration or belief pattern is serious about its job, which is to hold this image of you every time you look in the mirror. So when you find yourself up against another person for a job selection or promotion, would it seem likely that you would believe you'd get it? You may be the most qualified candidate, but if you resonate with the energy of being unwanted, others pick up that silent message in the form of an energetic vibration and respond to it without knowing why. Will you be the first one chosen for the basketball team or for a date on prom night? You can feel the answers because we have all known people who resonate like this and we can feel the unwantedness also. We may feel sorry for them, and want to help or save them, but we are powerless to change them. Only they can disempower the electricity (energy) that is fueling the vibrations that are limiting themselves.

Think of vibrations throughout the universe, everything has one. Whether it is a glass table or a piece of wood, a rock or an emotion, the color red or the color blue, they all resonate somewhere on the vibrational scale. Let's focus on emotions for a moment. Imagine going into the room of someone you know who may be depressed or sad. You immediately feel their vibration, even if they try to mask their mood from you, you automatically pick it up. You respond by feeling down yourself or wanting to go somewhere away from their energy. This is because you are connecting to them, matching their vibration. Some of us may want to help this person because we don't like the way they make us feel. Or we may want to just run away from the feeling. We deal in energy all day long without being aware of the underlying forces that make up our present selves. What if someone is angry and coming your direction ready to fight? You feel the anger even before they get close to you. It is a powerful energy and travels at a low, thick vibration. Your natural instinct will either be to get out of the way, or dig in and prepare for a fight. Either way, you have acknowledged the vibration of anger and prepared for it. You have been an energy worker your entire life without realizing it. We just haven't been trained in how to recognize and deal with energy in a beneficial way.

Imagine going to your grandmother's house when she is feeling sick and lonely and wants someone to hear her sorrows. She may be vibrating that day with "loss of support." She feels there's no one in her life that truly cares about her ills. You instinctively pick up the station she is broadcasting and either come to help support her, or retreat and quickly leave if you feel you are unable. Maybe you are having an energy deficit day and really don't have any energy left for grandma. Again you respond to this invisible energy and react accordingly.

Quite often we see couples where one person is predominantly strong and the other submissive. We either feel sorry for the submissive one and feel the overbearing one is being controlling, or feel that the submissive one is being pathetic and the strong one is being protective. Either way of seeing them may be accurate, but whichever view you ascribe to, it is simply an example of drawing the vibration that each person involved requires. If I feel that the world is out of control and seek to find personal control, I am going to be quite happy when I meet a nice, quiet and controllable mate. If I am submissive, or carry the mark of worthlessness, I may naturally draw to me a mate who is quick to make decisions for me and treats me as an inferior. It's what I expect anyway, right? On superficial analysis, the dysfunction is supported by the vibration.

But if we were to look deeper into their whole journey, or at least the part that is being activated by this relationship, we may find that both persons are going to challenge the other one in exactly the way that the other person needs most. We may see that the submissive can only stand being treated as an inferior for so long. In order to rise up against someone so domineering and controlling, they will have to muster more strength than they ever thought possible just to even be able to voice their own needs. It is just like when a mother whose child is trapped beneath a car finds the power of her adrenals and then proactively ignites them to collect the strength of 10 Goliaths! If you are a friend or relative watching a relationship like this during its learning phase, your advice may very well be, "get out!" If this is your reaction, you may not be seeing the whole picture. Go get some popcorn, settle back, relax, and wait for the story to unfold. They are probably both resonating with a sense of worthlessness and together will either teach each other this is an illusion, or they will find another way of learning it.

Often we think we are doing the best for our loved ones when we may very well be removing the challenges that create the tension of profound growth. I was talking with a woman the other day who asked me to assist her son who was in court for the custody of his children. She asked that I send some energy to his ex-wife's attorney to, essentially, help him overlook unwanted bits of slander about her son. I reminded her that this was not my job, nor would I suggest it. I suggested that if she felt compelled to assist energetically, she could send the energy of justice, which I assumed they all wanted. Knowing this young man, I could see that the trial had been a serious growing experience for him, even though it was extremely painful and difficult. He had always been very submissive and saw himself as weak. Standing up to his ex-wife, a woman capable of manipulation, control, and not easily intimidated, had forced him (at the cost of losing his children) to find his own hidden strengths. In front of a courtroom, he had to promote himself as an admirable father and capable caretaker, overcoming slander and gossip assumedly planted by his ex-wife's family. It is not an experience a mother wants to see her son go through, but it could very well be the keystone of his own self-worth. Once again, it is not our job to know what is best for someone else. Everyone has their own journey. To allow our loved ones to meet their own monsters can be very frightening to us, especially if they are our monsters too. To honor this process and to offer support is often the best we can do.

Energy healing, or healing of a person's soul happens by disconnecting them from the negative energy that is forming their particular reality. If we have the power to create our own realities which are negative or disempowering, then, guess what? We also have the power to recreate them as positive and empowering. First, we must become aware of what self-images we are vibrating with and which emotions are following us from relationship to relationship.

3 Understanding Differences

HOW WE COMMUNICATE

As humans we have this sophisticated tool called communication that is supposed to assist us while we are alive. But more often than not, it seems to fail us or get us into even more trouble. There are a slew of reasons why. Here are a few, and a few ways of understanding how to consciously move through these barriers.

One thing to keep in mind is this; we communicate with words only as much as we are verbally communicative people. Basically, we are not all the same when it comes to the act of communication. Each person has a different way of receiving and giving information.

Some people are *feeling* people. They process the world through their feeling sensitivities. Though not readily able to say what they are exactly feeling, they certainly are compassionate about sharing your troubles. They are the kind that will sit with you and cry, but may not know what to say. Sometimes they have trouble differentiating between their own emotional feelings, and what they have absorbed from someone else. They also may take a while longer than others to form words for their feelings while they are communicating. The man I have worked with for many years who has beautifully and artistically framed all my paintings is one such individual. When I first started working with him, I thought he was trying to put me off or didn't have time for me because he would never talk to me. So I would rush even more in my brief communications with him, and all the while he would barely utter a word. I took it personally until one day when I must have been in a particularly slow and laid-back mood, I asked him a question and then waited. I don't mean that I waited four or five seconds until he formulated his reply. I must have waited three or four minutes before he responded. But slowly, surely, came his well thought out, creative answer, amazing as it seemed to me. So ever since then, we have communicated in this way. He has an intuitive understanding of my work, and I have come to appreciate his subtlety. I realize that he would rather communicate without words if only we could. He truly is a *feeling* person.

Some people are *fire* people. Hit with intense emotion they let out the first thing they feel, even if it is inappropriate or insensitive. They are usually brutally honest. They feel things with intense emotion and have active brains. Mostly, they are like fire, burning hot and then, once the fire is out, or their interest wanes, they turn cold. These people are hard to communicate with in those first few moments after saying, "Dad, I wrecked your car." But if you can wait through their initial intense emotional reaction, you will find a good listener. It's just that most people can't make it through the first few flailing impassioned moments and may do anything to avoid conflict with this person. One thing to be aware of when engaging a fire person is they are not aiming their intensity at you for any other reason than you are in front of them and are providing a spark. That's just how they are, and if you can hold your ground calmly until the first bonfire of emotion has waned, you will usually find someone who can see logically and help come up with a reasonable solution. Unfortunately, they can be so intimidating that you may want to avoid them or try to find alternate ways to deal with them, sometimes even at your own expense.

My dad was like a fire person and when I was growing up I must have found a way to wait through his initial temper because all my other siblings (and sometimes even my mother) would ask me to petition our father on their behalf. I'd say, "*You* ask him yourself!" but they would convince me I was the only one he would say yes to. That wasn't actually the case. I was the only one who would *wait* for yes. After four or five adamant *no*'s, when he saw I was still there awaiting another response, he would start to become more logical. Then I could reason with him.

Other people are *practical* people. They tend to nonverbal communication. The fewer words the better. You all know someone like this: the stereotypical old farmer sitting out on the porch observing his roof being torn off by a tornado, still rocking in his chair. Later, you say, "Grandpa, why didn't you *do* anything?" to which he'd reply, "Nothin' to be done." You just need to understand that is how they are, it doesn't mean they are any more or less humane or caring, that is just how they communicate. These are the kind of people who go out into the yard and start chopping wood or tearing down the old shed when they are hit by grief or problems too big to wrestle. Trying to talk to them, or to comfort and communicate with them during stressful times is a bit like speaking to the proverbial brick wall. Better to wait until something has softened in them and their system is ready for external communication. The practical communicators can be somewhat frustrating to the more talkative individuals, but they are just made this way and have their own unique lessons to teach.

Lastly, there are *verbalizers*. These people talk and talk and keep on talking, long after they have explained themselves backwards and forwards. They specialize in communication, like to write letters, poetry, songs, keep journals or express themselves verbally. They are excellent communicators, but can come up short in the truly compassionate area. I have found that they love the art of communication. They like telling stories and sharing viewpoints, but often are just waiting until you have finished just to assert their own ideas again. They have a tendency to want to prolong a conversation or, some would even say, develop a discussion or even an argument just for the sake of being verbal and enjoying the art of speech and communication. They are usually pretty friendly, and so can connect verbally with more people, but sometimes others see them coming and if they don't have sufficient time, will detour to avoid them. They are in heaven with a group of people who listen to them, and who they can exchange thoughts with. It is the verbal volley they love. So when engaging with this type of communicator make sure you are connecting with the genuine article and not just listening to words for the sake of hearing the words spoken.

Imagine this scenario: you are a fragile young child trying to tell your mother that you have just had a really creepy experience at school, not really understanding if this type of thing is normal or not, and you are a *verbalizer*. You talk and talk, waiting for some sense of understanding, watching your mother's face but seeing no change or response. You describe the experience, verbalize your feelings, but still no reaction. You imagine that she is judging you or finds what you are talking about trite or stupid and not worth her time. You finally say, "never mind" and go to your room feeling embarrassed. Mother never says a thing. She is processing and thinking. You never actually asked her anything, so being a *practical* person, there didn't seem to be anything to say. She would have gladly responded and she certainly had an opinion she would have given had you actually asked. Given that interaction you may now have a mother and child who are think-ing two very different things about the same experience. Your mother prides herself in not prying or intervening in her growing child's life, but *you* are feeling that your mother couldn't be more compassionless and uncaring!

A woman I know was telling me about how she communi-cated with her son when he was in his young teens. They were very different and did not share the same thoughts on many things. She said whenever they tried to communicate it always ended terribly. She finally was introduced to a kind of therapy where they just sat face to face in chairs across from each other and looked at one another. She said they communicated more through those looks than in all the words they had ever tried to exchange. She said as soon as she would open her mouth, the communication she sought would all fall to pieces. I suggested that what she might have been conveying during her nonverbal exchange was her unconditional love for her son, for which there are really no words. As soon as she tried to understand her son or rationalize herself through words, the feeling of this beautiful love would fade.

There are many more ways to communicate with someone than with words (as I will suggest a little later), but the most im-portant thing is in attempting genuine understanding. If you can identify the key players in your life as one of these four types of communicators you will be *less* inclined to take their responses or lack of responses personally. And really, no matter what you try to convey in a conversation, the others' responses are theirs alone, and your responses to them are yours alone, not the other way around as people invariably try to convince us. Many times in a heated conversation when emotions are flying, you will be hit with, "you made me feel this way," or "you're making me be such and such undesirable trait." This is especially when you need to remember, *you are responsible for your emotions only.* How others respond to their own are their responsibility. How you respond to someone saying that you are a mean and selfish person, for instance, depends upon how much that comment vibrates with your core beliefs. If it hits a nerve, then your heightened emotional response tells you you have some work to do looking at why you feel you are a mean and selfish person. If you don't resonate with mean or selfish at all, that accusation would elicit very little response. It's like the adage, "What you think of me is none of my business." That is the ultimate in living the "I am responsible for my own responses only" approach.

Identifying yourself as one of these four types of communicators, or a variation of the four types, will also help you see how others see you. If you have the impetus, you will find a way to truly communicate and communication is the door to understanding.

MAGNETIC POLARITY

Much of my work centers around helping people understand their loved ones. One of the most important steps in this understanding is removing the judgment of good and bad when seeing others. People are a compilation of many complex options. Some of these we have already discussed, such as how people communicate, what karmic obligations they come with and how they are affected by their biology, personality and tastes. Now I'd like to introduce the concept that people can also be seen in terms of their magnetic polarity. It is like thinking of us as batteries. Batteries have a (+) on one end and a (–) on the other end. That does not make one end of the battery good or bad, each pole is a necessary component in the battery's function of storing energy. Some people operate energetically as either the negative pole or the positive pole. Our culture tends to lead us to believe that things *positive* are good and things *negative* are bad. I want to go beyond this way of thinking for a minute to see the (+) and the (–) as just two ends of a self-sufficient energy source. Not only does this take the judgment out of it, it helps us see that both are necessary. Just like in a battery.

If we can imagine that as souls we get to make some choices about who we are going to be in our physical incarnation, then choosing our polarity is one of our choices. I would assume that we make the choice that is consistent with our journey. Is it going to be light and fun loving or heavy and serious this time around? Either way, there are as many ways to express our true selves as there are souls that need expressing. Choosing negative or positive polarity is just one option on the list of possibilities that combine to make up each unique individual.

I really don't have to tell you much about both poles because they are so common. We all know people of both natures. But let's look at some common traits. Positively poled people tend to see the world in positive ways; in terms of possibilities, how to turn a difficult situation into a positive event. They tend to look on the optimistic side of life (the cup half full versus half empty). Some would even say that they are the more unrealistic daydreamers or that they are just setting themselves up for disappointment and disillusionment. But the positively poled person generally can make something acceptable out of even the most critical or stressful situation. The negatively poled person generally comes from "no." They are more skeptical, more leery of a good thing and are wary of those who are too optimistic. They can see the worst-case scenario in pretty much every situation and brace themselves for the worst that the world can throw at them. They consider themselves realists and don't find life too disappointing because they've already expected the worst possible outcomes beforehand. They can be easily depressed and judgmental.

All of us know people who fall, generally speaking, into one category or another. This does not make them bad or good people, it is just how they are, just as in the necessary two ends of a battery. The reason I bring this concept up as part of this book is because in working with people having relationship problems,

whether they are with teens or mates or parents or friends, it comes
down to people wanting to have the other person see things from
their own point of view. As the folksinger Ani DiFranco sings,
"and is it really the best we can do
to arm wrestle over whose world it's gonna be?
(the one according to you
or the one according to me)"

I taught a watercolor class at the university in my town last
semester and integrated my energy work (removing limiting beliefs) to help my students get rid of images of themselves that
were constricting their creativity. I truly loved teaching the class
and looked forward to it every week. Our class had really become
a place to express ourselves in every way. Then our country initi-
ated a war with the people of Iraq. The day that the war began
everyone in my class (29 students of all ages and persuasions)
came to school very animated and upset as would be natural given
the circumstances. I overheard before class some of their comments and found myself getting upset. I felt that they were simply
mimicking the media's interpretations as proposed on TV, and I
didn't want to hear any of it. I didn't want to not like these students I had grown to care for so much. We began the lesson, and
as they were all painting they continued discussing their various
viewpoints on the war. I still didn't want to hear it (theirs were so
far from my own opinions) that I shut them down. I said, "No
talking about the war." They became quiet and subdued and their
paintings reflected this expressive shut down.

The night before the next class was to meet, I was sitting in
my studio trying to decide what to do for the class session when
my husband came in. He said, "Are you having trouble with
tomorrow's class?" I admitted that I was torn up about shutting
my students' freedom of expression down at a time when they
obviously needed to vent. He did point out that I was the one
who created this atmosphere for open expression, and I couldn't
just choose when to let it come out and when to silence it. So he
suggested that I allow them to express themselves in a construc-

tive way about the war, and as he put it, art can be a social commentary. So the next day I began the lecture with a discussion of honoring others' opinions (as much to remind myself as for them) and that we were all going to paint something that expressed emotionally how we each *felt* about the war. Not how we think we ought to feel or how our parents or friends think we should feel, but emotionally how we each were responding to our country being at war. What they produced put me to shame. They each did something completely different and I realized as we positively critiqued the paintings at the end of class that there aren't just two ways of looking at a thing, that there are as many ways as there are brains that think and hearts that beat. I realized that I really did think they would be more evolved people if they shared *my* opinions. After I saw their works, I realized that it is far more complicated than that.

We as a class saw that no two people in that classroom shared exactly the same opinion, but by the end, after having been presented each piece by the artist, we were all more capable of honoring each other's differences. We didn't all fall into just two camps, those for and those against. The emotions evoked by the war were more subtle and confusing than that, especially to those who had friends fighting in Iraq. What I myself came to understand was that we all are complex individuals, and what a drone of an existence it would be if everyone shared my opinions only. In order for everyone to feel open enough to share these feelings we had to make a safe environment where emotions could be offered in a non-vulnerable way. Before we each shared our finished paintings, I made sure that everyone (including myself as the instructor) knew the importance of honoring each other's feelings. Opinions are personal and emotions are even more personal. When a person is offering their emotions, it is not appropriate to judge those emotions as right or wrong according to our own emotionally based opinions. Emotions are not right or wrong, they just are. Even snorting or heavy breathing at a critical moment can be interpreted as a hurtful response to our personal expression. Facial gestures and body language also express what our mouths do not, but are just as powerful. In the journey to understand each other and have interpersonal relationships, honoring what others say as well as honoring our own voices is highly critical.

In doing that, especially in the context of polarity, it is important to consider that other people may not come from the same viewpoint as you, or even the same magnetic inclination. Many of my clients want me to *fix* their spouses or children who always seem sad or unhappy or who don't seem to enjoy life as much as the concerned person thinks they could. My response is, "That is who they are, and you are attracted to them because they represent that opposite polarity much of the time." If we could think in terms of *choice* instead of what's better or worse, we wouldn't take on the burdens of those we love, we could just *honor* them. By choice, I mean, in a bigger way, before we came into our mother's bellies, before we got our present personality, before we got married or baptized. Choice, as in, "What do I want to ultimately express in this lifetime, as this being?" Those choices were made for a reason. I don't propose to know what these reasons are for everyone else, but I think somewhere, deep within ourselves, we intuitively know our own. So, when we think we need to fix negatively poled people, or bring positively poled ones down to earth, we are ultimately not honoring their own soul's choices.

I have observed some things about the two poles that I find useful in dealing with them. Negatively poled people tend to see things much in the way a minus sign functions. What does a minus sign do? It gives us the *difference* between two things. The difference between 10 and 2 is 8. That is also what these people tend to do. They identify the differences between people. That person is darker or lighter or shorter or richer or uses more natural resources than this person. That's why others tend to see these negatively poled people as judgmental. Perhaps part of their journey takes them into this realm, of understanding differences, hopefully for the purpose of eventually shining some much needed light on something they very passionately need to learn in this life.

Positively poled people do what plus signs do. They add together. They see the sum of two people, or of groups or things. That's why they tend to be more outgoing as well. They see definite advantages of joining efforts with others of particular personality types. They see the positive in people and want to meld efforts to a common goal. They may not see the differences, and only focus on the potentials. They enjoy parties where people of all types are together, sharing, being light, having joy. They see the sum of what these people could be together.

Now is it any wonder that positively and negatively poled people attract each other? They each have inherently what the other is missing. For example, my negatively poled husband has helped me on more than one occasion be prepared in business dealings where I was not suspecting anything but the best possible outcome to occur. In fact, I have had to follow his promptings many times to avoid being taken advantage of or dishonored. He also has enjoyed my lightness and joy in everyday living, something that does not come naturally to him.

In the case of child and parent, there is a tendency of the positively poled individual to want to make life better for the other. I have seen this with children towards a parent or parent to a child. It is a natural tendency either way. The parent thinks that they somehow are to blame for the sad behavior and depressed sociability of the child, that they did something wrong as a parent, and they want someone, anyone to make their child happier, more socially accepted and joyful. Or the child who is positive and lighthearted who sees his mother as being sad or pensive, also thinks that somehow his birth into her life has brought some sadness that she will not say. He thinks that if only he could do or say the right thing, she would find internal happiness. But guess what, it's nobody's fault. It was a choice. The sooner we can understand this, the sooner we can begin to honor each other's presence in our lives as exactly what it is, a gift, not an anchor.

A full understanding of the reasons why we choose to come into this life as one pole or another may be impossible for anyone to know, but at least I can offer some insights into some of the advantages of each and reasons one pole may accommodate our journey better than another. Let me start with the underdog, the negatively poled.

NEGATIVELY POLED

Many people think that if only they could get a certain change of attitude they would see life in a better light. But I think this is an important part of the journey of this life. In the case of my favorite negative polarity guy, my husband, his own life's suffering has greatly aided his ability to be a dynamic healer. Many of his patients know that he knows their pain without talking about it, because he has been there himself. He understands depression and the cycle of negativity that results. His genuine understanding and hopefulness at the same time give his patients much needed inspiration to overcome their own despair. So for him, the choice meant his own life would be less light or joyful, but his journey called for it. What he does for me in my life is adds contrast to my own journey's fabric. He casts the shadow behind the object to enhance it even more. He challenges my beliefs and creates enough tension that I must make decisions myself. I have to either hold on tightly or abandon my beliefs. From this daily challenge I know that in the face of the worst storm, I will not capsize.

When I look at young people, from a teacher's perspective, I have found some of the most profoundly creative to be negatively poled. They internalize, and as they go inward, come to face some very deep emotions. If properly equipped (encouraged and provided with a safe environment) the expression of this meeting can be very moving. Look at Chopin, a very sensitive, ill, depressive individual, and the passionate music he created. Nobel prize winner for literature, Knut Hamsen, created his most incredible works during a 10-year depression. Hemmingway, Dostoevsky, James Dean, I could go on. My point is to say that, possibly, our job as positively poled people in their lives is to look at their choices and help support them. If they have chosen to be antisocial, don't close off any other options, but allow them a private space to be what they need to be in order to feel at home somewhere. If they want to go inside themselves, help them by providing the desired instruments of creativity for this endeavor, whatever those may be. Remember that they need the opposite polarity for balance, so don't try to make them drink the whole antidote. They just need your positively poled energy for balance, not to reform them or fix them.

One of my dear friends is a gentle and sensitive negatively poled individual. She is inherently a loner and even though she likes the company of others, does not seek them out. She married a man who was the most positively poled person I know, probably even gives us positively poled people a bad name! After a few years of marriage she told me that he brought to her life all the excitement, entertainment and fun that she had ever thought about, but could not elicit herself. Almost every evening, he would bring someone home for dinner or invite a neighbor over, entertaining and enjoying the sum of them all! She watched and enjoyed and registered it all. Even though their journey was not long together, what he brought to her life stayed; the ability to open up and enjoy others when that may not have been her natural propensity. Now she has a more balanced life. Although much of it still lived in her own private world, she is able to be open and receptive to others and the joy they bring into her life. She has attracted a negatively poled man and now plays the role of the positive in her new relationship.

That brings me to a question I often get. Can a person change? Yes, since everything in the universe is changing, why not us? I would think that if the original reason that you created a particular personality attribute has now gone, or you have sufficiently learned the lesson from that attribute, then the reason for it being there in the first place would be gone as well. The same applies to relationships. People often ask me, how do you know if you have finished with a particular relationship and you should leave it, or you are just avoiding the reason they are there in your life and just *want* to leave? I have no idea. I leave that up to each individual's own wisdom. One thing I have been saying to myself mostly, but to my clients on occasion is, remember, this person you are having a challenge with is your *teacher* not your *torturer*. They may appear to be the latter if we are looking through the lens of our ego only. Bring the soul's larger wisdom in and we see, "ah, that guy is a teacher, created especially for me!" Our children and parents are even more so, they are related and thus may be more physically/genetically bonded.

To hold out that a person will change is not honoring their journey, however. Whether someone changes or not is part of their own particular destiny, but the form they show up in at your doorstep is the reason they are in your life. So I suggest not dwelling on getting someone to change, but instead learn to accept and honor that individual exactly as they are. It truly takes the weight off of you as the responsible party (in your mind at least) since it is not your place to bring the imperative joy or dutiful realism into another person's life.

POSITIVELY POLED

Now let's look at the positive polarity individual. After all that deeply creative and sensitive caring stuff of the negatively poled, we positive people can sometimes feel somewhat superficial. I did not mean to imply that positive people are party animals and beach bums. What they bring to this world is a lighter outlook, another way of seeing a thing in a different light. "*Look,*

I still have one lens left in my glasses! That crashing wave didn't take them BOTH!" While the balancing partner is on the beach looking on, thinking, "Whoa, what bad luck, my friend got his glasses all broken up and now they are useless." The positively poled person brings that feeling of hope, even in the light of catastrophe. They find joy in the mundane things of life, in the smallest, most obvious. They find the enthusiasm to begin again after many failures. They see the beautiful red sunset as a grace of nature, and not the pollution haze of man that created the red color.

I lived near the Ohio River when I was growing up and a friend of mine and I used to go there in the evening to just sit and enjoy the sound of the water and watch the boats. Well, I did, anyway, I think he just went with me. He would always point out all the trash that had washed up along the river's edge since we were last there. I had never noticed it before. The river was always so nurturing for me that I only noticed what felt wonderful to me. What would I have done if I had noticed the debris? Would I have seriously undertaken the task of cleaning the Ohio River, the second longest river in the United States? Probably not, as a teenager. His comments and my responses to the same pollution were just a result of the way we were inherently poled. He couldn't help seeing it anymore than I could not see it.

Positive polarity individuals are more accepting, after all they see the sums, they see themselves in that sum. So, what's to judge? How much fun can one person have? Too much? Never! Positively poled people are the ones at the other end of the phone who happily promise they will get to the problem of your customer dissatisfaction. Whether they do or not depends on if they have a negatively poled person actively participating in their life, bringing responsibility and a healthy amount of skepticism. Still, you enjoy hearing the enthusiastic voice of the positive. These are the people who bring youthful enthusiasm to any project or idea, no matter how impractical it may seem. After all, dreams are the beginnings of things not yet discovered or still thought to be impossible. Perhaps these pertly poled ones laugh more and tell more jokes and find humor in more things, but maybe they are just more poised to be light. Either way, you can see that it takes both kinds to make the world go around. Essentially, if we honor who we have chosen to be, even if we aren't done yet, and we honor others, even if they are on a different journey than ours, we will have immensely more fulfilling relationships with others as well as with ourselves.

4 Identifying Similarities

There is a mythological story of a boy named Narcissus who went around gazing at the reflection of himself in a clear pond because he liked what he saw. He thoroughly enjoyed the view that greeted him every time he caught a glimpse of himself in something that reflected. The term narcissistic has come to represent someone who is overly proud of his physical appearance. But turn back the pages to when Narcissus first came to see himself, he was probably amazed at how beautiful he appeared in contrast to how he thought of himself inside. So he was pleasantly pleased to find an attribute that was redeeming. If he already had an image of himself that was beautiful, why would he have constantly stared at himself after discovering the reflective surfaces of nature?

EQUAL SOULS

If there's one thing I have found that consistently applies to all of us, in doing my energy work, it is that souls are beautiful. Everyone's soul is a perfect reflection of divinity. However, we, as humans, seem to find it necessary to heap all sorts of ugly, untrue images on top of that natural reflection until we can no longer see or remember the beauty of our own souls.

As James Hillman suggests in his book *The Soul's Code*, the equality mentioned in the Declaration of Independence of the United States wherein "all men are created equal" most likely refers to the *soul's* equality. It is quite evident that we are all physically and materially dissimilar, but the soul and the freedom of those souls are what is equal in all. I believe that the fabric that created all our souls was laid out across the universe and each of us was cut from the same bolt of cloth, and that cloth is divinity. Many do different things with their piece of material, just as each individual tailor would. But that is what we are doing here, expressing the Divine in the unique way that only we, with our own set of traits, personality, karma, talents, and biology can do. If we express ourselves wholly, then we are expressing the Divine in yet another incredibly miraculous feat of nature.

WHAT AM I REACTING TO THAT IS MINE?

One young man I know who comes from a very loving and supportive family, now that he has reached young teenhood, has begun to challenge his father to the very limits. Up until this point he was what everyone who knew him would have called the perfect child. Now suddenly, without intention, he is being a serious challenge to his father. His father is a very conservative, strong-willed, hard working person. As long as his son was doing all the things he found important in life, life was bliss for them all. However, the individuating process began and no one could go back in time to undo it. Our young man, Nelson, is not inherently like his father at all. He is intuitive, highly compassionate, and deeply feeling. Not to say that his father isn't a compassionate man, he just doesn't value the promotion of those qualities. Now let's stop and take a look at the bigger picture, from the perspective of the Universe and the concept of soulful evolution. What a brilliant choice these two made to come into each other's lives, to bring and share the qualities that the other did not possess. Seems like a grand idea, right? When you are looking through the lens of the soul, yes, but when you look through the lens of the ego, it becomes a different story.

This is where we exist in this life, on the material or egoic plane. Our souls certainly exist on this physical plane as well, but the main emphasis in our world is on the material, or what you can see and touch. In this example, we have Nelson and his father. You can picture the scene. Nelson decides he does not really want to become a competitive professional tennis player (like his father has encouraged), but would like to pursue his interest in the piano, and not competitively, but for enjoyment. When the father, John, sees he can help further his son's interest in the piano, he suggests lessons from a more brilliant teacher to encourage competitive piano abilities. Nelson then quits the piano altogether. John sees this as a personal power confrontation. Nelson wants to see what it is his father is really about. Subconsciously, Nelson is asking why his father is so stuck on the idea of becoming a competitor. In the heat of a family discussion, guided by his own intuition (which we all have access to, by the way) Nelson says something like, "Maybe *you* should be the athlete or world class pianist, if only you *could*." Wow! Uh-oh, that strikes a nerve in John that sends him into an emotional frenzy, aimed at Nelson, while we, as observers, have already figured out that the entire dynamic has to do with John's unfulfilled desires for himself, not his son.

In a highly evolved family situation, the father would realize his unfulfilled desires to complete whatever goals he had set for himself before marriage, children and responsibilities. He would then find a healthy way (marathons, renewed lessons or refocusing of these goals) to find what he himself was searching to complete, not through his son, but though himself. However, if family dynamics were evolved to that level, transcendent of human emotions, there would be no need for a book like this. So, suffice it to say, the majority of us live by the trial and error method. Think about it, if we stored our unresolved issues up in the attic in the first place, there was probably a really good reason. Relooking at them is not going to be easy, but more likely painful.

The truth is, the Nelson and John scenario is still going on. Challenging, threatening, pouting, withdrawing, stalemate, challenging, discussion, giving in, rebelling and so on. Eventually, one of two things will happen. John will understand why he pushes his son so hard, but it won't be the answer he has been giving himself all this time of wanting the best for his son and wanting to make him a strong and competitive individual in a harsh dog-eat-dog world. Or he will spend some time in self-reflection asking why Nelson is pushing his buttons. Something deep within his spiritually evolving self may ask, "Do I need to listen to his unspoken message, of integrating his way with my way? Is there another way than to force my will on others? Is there a way to honor what Nelson wishes and still teach him some of my ethics and values?"

What I am suggesting is trying to identify in each relationship what is yours and what is theirs. Many years ago I remember someone who really got me thinking along these lines. We were carpooling from the overcrowded North Bay into the heart of the City. It was a delight to have someone to talk to during the long and sometimes tedious drive as well as have access to the carpool lane. One day, my carpool buddy told me his wife had demanded that he stop carpooling with me, that it was the stuff affairs were

made of. I was shocked, this had never been anything but a pla-
tonic relationship. I didn't know what to say. Then he said, "I told
her that was her own fear and it wasn't mine and that she needed
to deal with it, and I intend to continue carpooling." Wow, that
seemed somewhat insensitive when I first thought about it, but
he obviously wasn't interested in upholding an emotionally in-
dulgent misbelief. He had never acted inappropriately and I didn't
suspect he ever would. He was someone of strong integrity, and
by continuing his car-pooling, he demonstrated to his wife that
he was not going to entertain a relationship with her that supported her fears.

In looking at similarities, a basic human need is that we all
want to be heard and we want someone to accept our opinions as
valid and concrete. But we become embroiled in a game of either/
or. My opinion is right and yours is wrong, or yours is right and
mine is wrong. It is like the guy who wonders, if he's the only one
in the forest, without a woman for miles, is he still wrong? It's sad
to even have jokes like this, but it elucidates the either/or game.
This is simply the epitome of a stalemated lesson. The journey
isn't about going the right or the wrong way, but about *how* you
do the trip. I come back to the concept that opinions are like
emotions, they are neither right nor wrong, they are just what
they are, opinions. To begin to honor that another may have a
different opinion, like my watercolor class on war day, is to begin
to open yourself to the reason someone is in your life. Once you
have stepped aside from the either/or, win/lose game you begin to
access something divine.

AUTHORITY FIGURES AS EQUAL

It is here I want to address relationship issues with those you
have chosen to have authority over you, whether it is the boss of
your current job, your father, mother, or someone from a religious or social organization you are plugged into. What I want to

remind you is just that, you have *chosen* that person or persons to have authority over you. You have accepted something about what they have to offer you and you have placed them on a higher shelf than the one you reside on. There are two things to remember here. First, all souls are equal and therefore this person whose 'name cannot be named' is simply commanding more power in this physical incarnation, but to the Infinite, you are exactly the same, plodding along your own unique journey with equanimity. Secondly, all souls inherently know they are equal and will eventually send vibrations of resentment if held in an unequal position for too long. You may find yourself at various stages in this situation, but just reminding yourself that they may hold an earthly title that society defers to over yours, and that you ultimately hold the key to your own self-esteem, will help you move through the stagnation and resentment created by this type of relationship. It is about allocating power again. Energy is power and when you have given someone your power by allowing them authority over you, you have given them part of your own individual energy. That is why many organizations are so powerful, it is not one man or two, it is the compilation of many people's energy or power given willingly to the organization.

PARENTS AS AUTHORITY FIGURES

I have worked with many people who defer to their parents even long after childhood. They hold back what they want to say and do what their parents want them to do because they feel obligated. Or they feel their parents' judgment on them because they still defer to them (consciously or not). The parent convinced them, undoubtedly from a very young age, that they were the all knowing, wise one, to establish the power differential in the parent/child relationship. Giving our power is easier than retrieving it. We may spend the better part of a life trying to become equals with our parents, waiting for them to gracefully say, "You have been good, you deserve to be trusted and I believe that you can make decisions wisely yourself." Rarely does that day ever come.

It comes down, again, to unraveling the *treasure* in this relationship. To have a challenging parent means they are going to be in your face (as in, related to you until you die) until this lesson is adequately received, providing the necessary tension needed to springboard us in our soul's desired direction. This dynamic requires that, undoubtedly after reaching the saturation point, you manifest the internal strength required to *demand,* nay, *command* your own power to return with confidence and authority. And maybe those were the exact traits your soul needed you to embody for you to truly take charge of your own destiny. Usually we find that our parents never really wanted the responsibility of caretaking our personal power anyway, but were going to hang on to it, feeling that we might need them to help live our life. We are just younger in physical age than our parents, but we are made of exactly the same divine cloth, equal as souls, divine in nature. Oftentimes we confuse the need for physical survival as reason for deferment, long after we are self-sufficient or certainly capable of being. I will talk later about exactly how to locate these particular issues and what we can do about them.

Essentially, how we are similar is that not only are our souls equal, but we have equal opportunity to access divine wisdom, universal love, information, intuition, guidance, and power. That, I believe, is our birthright. Much of the inequality on this plane exists because some of us know, and some of us don't, that we have this birthright.

We all want to be heard, accepted and loved. This is a human trait that everyone has a right to pursue. Many times what we see, with our human eyes, looking through the personally tinted glasses of our own perceptions, are a lot of egos running amuck, but everyone is searching in their own unique way towards the love and acceptance and happiness that their soul whispers to them is their birthright.

SUBTLE BODIES AT WORK

This brings me to another way we are all alike. That is that while we exist on the physical plane, we are endowed with an ego. I do not use this term as do the Buddhists, as something that needs to be *extinguished* in order to find happiness, but as a part of us that we must understand in order to *integrate,* and thus find happiness. I like to describe the ego as the personality. It is the face on our soul's body. It helps us cope with the living thing, keeping us alive, spurring us to succeed in a social way, avoiding mishaps that could cause embarrassment, and reminding us of our own limitations (the ones with which we came preprogrammed). The ego is not a bad fellow to hang out with, the problem comes when it is given full reign of the self and then its concern is for the issues of the ego only.

I see the self as a collection of entities, all of which together comprise what we call 'me', and none of which could operate alone. These entities are called the subtle bodies. They include the etheric, emotional, mental, egoic, karmic and soul bodies and hold information about us energetically. The *etheric* is that energetic part of you just outside your physical body that holds the pattern of your physical self. If you damage a knee in an accident, your physical body simply looks at the blueprints from the etheric body and makes the necessary repairs, like new. When the material self dies, the etheric goes with it.

The *emotional* body is that part of your energetic system that holds information about you depending upon how you feel. It carries weight for you through its capacity to feel and sense things. If you give it too much reign, it practically incapacitates the owner from an overabundance of differing emotions. If you don't allow it any participation, you may feel numb and insensitive.

The *mental* body's department includes those things you may have read or understood as fact, or been taught. There are those who put major clout in what is provable with the five senses, understandable, given logic as we Westerners know it, and perceivable with the mind. These people have given the mental body dominant rule over their energetic selves.

The *karmic* body is that part of you that stores pertinent information from previous places, realms or existences. I refer to this information later in the book as *baggage* we come into this life with.

The *ego* is the part of you that holds information energetically about who and what you believe you are. It has gathered societal hints, understood substructures and observed many lives. From these experiences, the ego body, as I said earlier, relegates itself to the job of protecting, advancing, promoting and differentiating this ego body from others.

The *soul* body, as I call the core of you or the essential you, is that part of you that I see as the wisest part of all the bodies, carrying divine wisdom, patient, knowing the bigger picture and willing to wait (sometimes), not pushy, but occasionally (luckily) unyielding. I trust this part of me to make the major decisions in my life. How do I get it to do that when the ego body *is* pushy and wants its way and is demanding and sometimes obnoxious? That's the hard part. The ego body is really not a bad part of you, it is not an evil seed, it just has a different set of goals, all of which have to do with this physical existence. That is where the soul and the ego bodies have differing opinions. The soul knows that sometimes the best thing for your journey is to exit out of this incarnation and regroup on the spiritual plane and carry on its tasks somewhere else, but the ego would never agree to that and will literally fight tooth and nail to keep the incarnated, physical self alive.

VISUALIZING THE SUBTLE BODIES

What works for me in maintaining relationships with my own subtle bodies is visualization. I imagine this character, my ego, and I know it wants certain things to happen. I also know that they are not always in accordance with my highest good, so I simply treat it like the immature entity that it is, immature in the sense of a child who always wants its own way. I try not to punish it, that never really works anyway, but instead speak with it in nurturing tones and ask kindly for it to submit its will to our wise friend, the soul. I speak of wise in the sense of an old person with infinitely more experiences. That if it will allow the soul to guide what we do, *we all* will have more fun, be more well thought of and really get everything we want. The reward for the ego is that it gets to reap the benefits of the soul's wiser decisions. When I am doing something, like my healing sessions, where I really cannot be influenced by the desires of my ego, I make sure before I start that it is safely off with something else to do and *not* in the captain's chair (his favorite place). What I have found works is to make friends with all the many aspects of oneself, but not to feel segregated or fractionated. It is like identifying the ingredients of your favorite dish. If you know exactly what to add to enhance a certain flavor or what to subtract when you need to tone the spices down, you can make subtle changes with the result being a dish that is more scrumptious and satisfying.

Years ago, when I started working with subtle bodies, I was having a hard time singling out one or differentiating between my own egoic motives and my attempt at getting more in touch with my own soul. I was consciously trying to bring awareness to my soul body to allocate more resources at that level. The way that finally worked for me was that as I began to find the characteristics of the various subtle bodies, each one took on a personality which allowed me to identify them with a character I already knew, an archetype really, so that I could have a more cognizant relationship with each one.

The most vocal of my bodies was my ego body, as may be the case with many people, and immediately he came through the mental fog as Capt. James T. Kirk, captain of the Starship Enterprise. This name is pretty familiar to most households in America, from the old television series *Startrek*. That image wasn't really a surprise, but I knew I had my work cut out for me if I was going to get *him* out of the captain's chair. That was his identity, that was who he *was*! I also knew I had a great ally if I needed strength and courage. I then put familiar characterizations to my other subtle bodies. The mental body became Jane Hathaway, the secretary assistant to the obnoxious little banker on television's *Beverly Hillbillies*. My emotional body was played by the movie actor, Forrest Whittaker, as the extremely emotional empath employed to locate the missing creature in the movie *Species*. My karmic body has just been making itself known and hasn't been cast yet. My soul body has no movie caricature that it can even remotely resemble. It is simply a beautiful radiant light, like the sun coming over a mountain in the morning. It is brilliant and all encompassing and truly divine.

I found it interesting that three of my subtle bodies are represented for me by old TV characters or movie stars even though I personally haven't had a TV for almost 20 years. I guess our early childhood years make quite an impression. Other people I know who have tried this visualization exercise and shared the results with me locate animals and imaginary characters too. If looked at archetypically, which is as a pattern or a model for a larger, symbolic type, then the tangible images may help us take one more step towards self-awareness. In fact, I was hesitant to share them, it seemed pretty personal information, but I felt like it would be helpful, if not amusing.

So now that you have a relationship with the various parts of yourself, you don't want to play favorites or get them into any kind of segregation or competition. This does not facilitate harmony. You want to try to create a feeling of a loving, caring family unit, all necessary for the journey we have ahead of us. No one gets killed (even though you feel like it sometimes) and no one gets more accolades than the others. Remember, each is important, with one distinction: the soul body has the final word. After a while, with positive results, you'll see how cooperative everyone will be in letting the soul body make all the really hard decisions. It also gets the others off the hook, so to speak. It is helpful for me to simply take a quick glance at my subtle body family (a picture is worth a thousand words) and immediately get a sense of what is happening in my energy system. If Kirk is sitting in the captain's chair, I know I am in for trouble. If the emotional body is weeping uncontrollably on the floor, I have work to do. If the soul body is nowhere to be found, I go to code red.

The hard part is communicating with the soul part of oneself. Different people have different ways. I use a form of meditation and visualization, but the key is finding that subtle high vibration and tuning in with it. That is a text unto itself. I am simply trying to offer ways of identifying what you're working with and what you may be interacting with in another person. I believe that we connect with others soul to soul. If we all had our heads lobbed off, we could still connect with others. It is a soul-code vibration thing. Everyone has had times when you've met someone and you feel like you've known them forever and other times, try as you might, you just could not make contact, find that sweet spot, jive, connect, or whatever with that other person. We as humans connect, vibrationally, soul-to-soul. Now if the person you are trying to connect with has his ego playing the role of the door-man, your soul may be saying the right password, but the door-man will not let your soul come in. In other words, you may want to connect in a genuine and openly trusting way, but the ego is just throwing clichés at you, operating behind a smoke screen, avoiding real subjects and only flattering the personality, anything to keep you from seeing the fragile, genuine soul article inside. I knew a woman like that. Every once in awhile in what felt like a genuine connection, I got to see that beautiful soul child, innocent and divine, but the rest of the time this very annoying bouncer would greet me at the door and not let as much as a big toe in.

WHO IS IN CHARGE HERE?

Let's look at specific occupations. Some careers nurture a stronger ego or brain or physical body, for example, than others. Politicians, for the most part, seem to be operating with the ego in the driver's seat, looking for personal power and material prestige. The way our society is set up, those with the desire to lead and to make rules and govern others choose the political path. This does not mean politicians are not intelligent or physically fit, it simply suggests that to follow this livelihood, one must strengthen the egoic muscles. You need personal power and the audacity to use it to get very far in the political world. Unfortunately, I think this is why we are sorrowfully lacking in leaders who exude confidence and integrity (things that the *soul* should be guiding). Instead, we have encouraged and allowed those who are very much in touch with what their personalized, strong egos want. They are allocating most of their resources to the immediate gains of the ego body. Those who are what I would call more balanced would not last long in our present egoically dominated political system. Movie stars and play actors also place their ego in the primary category of control, as a general rule.

I work a lot with professors, since I am in a university town, and find one thing they have in common is that their mental body is sitting quite fixedly in the captain's chair. They have invested lots of time and money into cultivating this icon of the mind and fully expect it to pay off. Usually the reason I am seeing them is because it isn't. They have doctorates, have written journal articles, published books, are well known in their fields, but they still feel unwhole. They are trying to understand life from the viewpoint of the brain, logically, proving what they believe, disregarding the rest. Part of it is that they are trying to get there, wherever there is, through one vehicle only, the brain. And as you have probably already figured out, you will be needing whatever vehicles you can beg, borrow or steal to make it through this journey we call life.

There are also those I call *emotionally self-indulgent*, probably they communicate as feelers, and have definitely spoiled their emotional child to the point of rotten! They hold others emotionally hostage and manipulate with the threat of an emotional outburst. Again, we see an imbalance in the individual's energy system. The same goes for those who have chosen a career path that demands a physically fit body over everything else. Whether they are professional athletes or make a living helping others stay fit, this is the part of themselves they have chosen to strengthen. These people do triathlons for fun! Maybe they are accountants by day and muscle builders at night, if they have allocated their primary resources to the physical body, this is the lens from which they view the rest of the world.

As I have alluded to earlier, you only have control over your own responses, not others'. So what happens when you find you are overwhelmed with people in your life who are definitely dominated by their ego, for example? Do you give up and do it their way, ego to ego? Do you get new friends, move to a different country, get a new boss? Do you let them have their way, butting heads and getting head injuries? You could. Or you could look at yourself again and ask, "Why am I so inundated with egoic personalities in my life right now?" From that question, you will find why they are there. Remember, there are no coincidences, everyone is in your life for a reason, even if it is rather annoying at the time. I also do this with astrology. I have studied astrology for many years and when three or more of a particular sign show up in my life at any one time, I ponder, what is *this* about? What are the particular attributes of this sign that I need to absorb now?

Is this group of egoic personalities lighting up or instigating an undue amount of negative emotions in me that through closer scrutiny could lead me to an unwanted personal trait? Am I ready to look at a way of being that requires less input from my own ego

body and more from my soul? Am I being upset by these pomp-
ous people because I carry some of these same attributes and they
are becoming obviously antiquated for my spiritual journey? It is
the same with all of us. If it were an easy task, we would have
gotten it long ago. Looking at our own process is the most difficult of all. I am pretty hard headed myself. I seem to get shown
my lessons in threes. My current goal is to try to get my life lessons on the second time around, instead of the third!

Mostly, reflect on yourself more than you scrutinize the other
party in a relationship. You can't do anything about them, you
can only do something about you. All the energy you put in to
trying to comprehend someone else's thought process or motivation is simply wasted energy, better spent somewhere else. If you
truly want to know someone, let them share with you, don't specu-
late. Coming through the ego filter, we most often imagine ourselves as a more key player than perhaps we truly are. "Hey, maybe
all that stuff I am worrying about that Joe said has absolutely
nothing to do with me." Can the ego deal with that truth? I offer
all these ways of looking at others not for the purpose of differen-
tiation, but for understanding. If you can believe that is just how
someone is set up right now, there are three benefits for you. It
takes the personalness out of the situation, hopefully eliminating
lots of unnecessarily hurt feelings. It allows you to situate yourself
however you need to be heard and understood from their perspective. And it leaves room for change on all sides.

Anyway, whoever (Kirk or Jane) you've got in you, or whatever (lions or tigers or bears), we all identify and allocate energy
differently to each part of us uniquely. In the meantime, we are
being who we are and reacting and responding to what others
presently are. That is the point and topic of this book. It is not to
be taken personally if you operate from the mental plane and you
cannot get someone who is operating from the emotional plane
to accept what you are saying simply because you can prove it.
They won't put much clout in your theoretical proof if they can't

feel it intuitively. Also, if you work with people in an industry where the ego is king, stand back, you will either have to match their ego (play their game with their ball) or perhaps not be understood, acknowledged or honored.

When you run into someone who is balanced in all areas of their life, you *feel* it. It feels like going home. There are no walls to scale, no barbs to avoid, no bouncers to get around, no muck to wade through, they are just whole and filled with a joyful light that gives you hope that this journey isn't for naught. If you know someone who exudes the kind of light and balance that comes from seeing the world equally from their wholeness, with their soul in the director's chair, keep their image in your mind's eye for inspiration. Meanwhile, Kirk and I duke it out! By the way, I am fortunate because I have shared my characters with my closest friends and they kindly remind me when Kirk has gotten back in the captain's chair. It's a much nicer way than saying, "You're being self-centered!" Watch Kirk *then!*

PERSONALIZED SUNGLASSES

One last thing about similarities is our own unique perceptions. Aside from our own ways of communication, and which part of us is presently in charge, we have our own way of looking at things. This is a similarity in that each of us has unique perceptions, and a difference because they are all different. To be aware of them is wise, to be able to understand them is probably impossible. Unless you have walked where another has, you can only view life from your own vantage point.

If you have pets or know any animals intimately, you will find out very quickly that they have preferences and they will make them known *tout de suite*. You think all dogs are alike? Try hanging with a dozen one day. My sister has one fish. Do fish have feelings? She swears that this fish prefers to be fed by her and not her husband. Now, I ask you, what about the multidimensional complicated self-aware human being? We're in huge trouble.

Where do preferences come from? Upbringing? To some extent. Genetics? To some extent. Karma? To some extent. The alignment of the stars at the moment of birth? To some extent. The color of one's hair? To some extent. Shall I go on? My point is we all come prepackaged with our own unique set of beliefs and preferences and likes and dislikes. I remember asking someone why they didn't like chocolate and they said, "Gee, same reason other people don't like spinach, I guess, it just doesn't appeal to me." They had a point, however difficult I found trying to comprehend not liking chocolate. Tastes are opinions, and remember what opinions are? They are personal and allowed, neither right nor wrong. When it's a taste for food, sometimes you can cut someone slack if it's something you don't really like either. But when it comes to beliefs in God and the Universe and love and trust and democracy and capitalism, then little wars break out. And Big Wars too, like the Crusades and the Inquisition and World Wars and Cold Wars, every kind of war, actually. So it would seem that itty-bitty relationships would be affected by these differences of opinion too…maybe. Probably. Later I will offer suggestions that actually assist in physically managing differences of opinion. But for now it is enough to say, all of us come packaged with what is technically termed our junk and no one's junk is more right than another's. Everyone sees the world through their own perceptions. We can choose theirs, or not.

5 Intelligent Dark Energy

OPERATING IN A NEGATIVE SPACE

At this point, I need to introduce an understanding of the energy of people who exist in a negative or detrimental space. When we are feeling angry or annoyed or worthless or unloved, or any one of a host of negative emotions we are all prone to, we let in negative energy. Think of these negative energies as real beings, like birds or bacteria. They are present, they just aren't visible. They exist as part of the earth/human school and the reason I bring awareness to them is because they can seriously compromise our ability to be balanced and serene and in a loving attitude. Negative energies seriously jeopardize our ability to maintain a loving and joyful relationship. Being aware of their presence, or even that they exist, seriously assists you along your journey, alone and together.

These energies are not demons in the biblical sense, but operate somewhat like that. Look at history and how each culture
evolved to include some mythical (or not) nymph, dybbuk, lepre-
chaun, genie, chimera, gnome, pixie or unnamed spirit capable of
mischievous deeds. They appeared in our human history for a
reason. Energies of a negative force exist. Even though they themselves are not to be feared, what they create in us does have elements of fear involved. Negative energy, or intelligent dark energy, has a job just like the rest of us, and that is to live and exist
and procreate. Their only way to procreate, or populate their own
kind, is to get *you*, the host, to open a door for them in yourself
and in the people around you. They feed off of our negative energetic emotions. That's it, quite simply put. When we generate a
host of mean thoughts or dark feelings towards others or especially towards our own selves in the form of self-hate, we are fixing up a delectable feast for these entities. How do we do this? We
as energy beings have, as the essence of us, certainly, more than
our physical bodies.

THE ENERGETIC BODY

If you could visually see your energetic body, it would look
something like a cocoon or oblong egg shape around the outside
of your physical body, extending perhaps as much as 10 feet or
more in each direction depending upon the person. This cocoon
of energy is not always solid, it has tears and holes in it, depending again upon the individual and their current state of awareness
and emotions. If you can believe that sometimes your physical
body is temporarily host to bacteria and foreign germs, then imagine your energetic body is also occasionally being host to energetic, or nonphysical germs. Just like with your physical body, if
you have overextended yourself, burning the candle at both ends,
not getting enough sleep and not eating well, you are usually more
prone to getting sick. When you are healthy and sleeping well

with relatively little stress in your life, your body usually responds with greater overall health.

Our energetic bodies operate much the same way as our physical bodies. If we are living in a space of love and joy with no stress (don't we wish?), our energetic cocoons are free of holes or tears and support us as a protected and respected being. Conversely, when we are feeling foul and upset and hateful, our energy cocoons are more like energy cobwebs, letting in many entities that feed off our substance and letting out our precious human energy. Ever say, "I feel *so* drained"? Sure you have, and that is exactly what is happening. Your energy system has a leak, or holes in it and many entities in our existence take advantage of that potential nutrition. The energy that powers a human, as well as an animal, is very potent and coveted. It is life-force energy, the essence that powers every living thing in the universe. It is very precious and special. Just like when we see a dead carcass on the side of the road, it isn't there long before the ants begin to work on it, then the birds, then the buzzards. Strange as it may seem, we are no different, we possess the most precious quality of all; life giving, divinely created energy. Is it any wonder that other beings want it?

OUR DOORWAYS

The door to your energy system is opened when you begin resonating with a heavy or negative vibration, such as self-hate or anger or resentment. *How* does intelligent dark energy enter? It is simply that the spheres of our energy-selves are not complete, they have gaping holes and the dark energy simply walks in. But they are not content with just feeding off of one host, they excel at multiplying. The way they do this is by accessing what I call *organic wisdom*, which is something we access all of the time, without knowing it. It is the information of what is, what has happened, and the energy of what we all broadcast and carry around with us in our baggage. It is where we gather intuition. It is what we're accessing when we feel something bad is about to happen. It is something that the rest of nature knows about and uses for its very existence. But organic wisdom is something most of humanity has forgotten how to access. We all feel the compelling drive, destructive as it is, to do it alone, to figure things out ourselves. Not knowing we have this infinite library of information to help us with all our decisions, we have historically chosen the route of least support, probably from many years of misinterpreting our own experiences. But we will deal with this more in detail later.

The main thing is that this intelligent dark energy is quite easily and guiltlessly accessing your information and mine and using it against us to further its own existence. They are very much like the intelligent life of bacteria, which alter their very cells to change in response to our human created antibiotics. Bacteria seek to survive in this world at our expense; dark energies seek the same goal!

MULTIPLYING

Ever been in one of those doozy arguments where things start to go really bad and then get even worse and then one person pulls out all the stops and says *the* thing that hurts you most in the world? It really stings. Whatever was said hurts enough to make you retaliate with an equally destructive comment. Later, you say, "What would make me say such a mean thing, that wasn't me talking?" Well, I'll tell you what, it was the dark energy that was operating through you. This intelligent dark energy is supplying you with exactly the right (or wrong, really) words to say at exactly the right (or wrong) time to elicit the most intense negative response, to increase the dark energy or emotion between all the parties concerned. Flip Wilson's comical old adage "the devil made me do it," is really not too far from an accurate assessment of what may be happening. I am just letting you know, even though we, as humans, are the action verbs and make the ultimate decisions, we have energetic assistance of which we should intelligently be aware. So, buying into this possibility for a moment, let's assume that quite often when we are pushed into our respective corners, some negative emotions light up, alerting this darker energy. We are not dealing with the inherent compassion of our soul at the controls during times like these. Where do you think the outcome of *any* conversation in which these intelligent dark entities are present would lead us? Down that road of creating more negative emotions. You might think you can reason with someone so negatively compromised. Believe me, you can't, we've all tried. It does not work. Once someone becomes so engulfed with dark energies they do not care about logic or reason. They only care about what will affect you the most, what will get you to open the door for the dark energies to come in. The negative energy that has compromised them needs you to become compromised as well. They beat you down until you also get angry and try to overpower the conversation all the while feeding the negativity. Or maybe you simply want to run away, only to seethe in the negative feelings left from the altercation. They win either way. The negativity has spread and grown.

Imagine this scenario. You plan to meet your friend for lunch and are in somewhat of a hurry, but want to keep your promise. You know you'll probably enjoy yourself once you get there and start talking. You wait 10, then 15 minutes, and finally your friend waltzes into the restaurant, not a care in the world. You're a little peeved because you need to get back to work. You have just wasted 15 minutes, not counting the travel time to the restaurant, and your friend doesn't even look repentant. You make some comment expecting an apology or at least an acknowledgment of your waiting. What you get back is more along the lines of, "What's bugging *you*?" As if it is somehow *your* fault for this sour mood. You make another comment, this one a little more cutting, hoping to scratch the skin. You're playing with the dark energy, let-

ting it work for you, and it makes the ego feel powerful. It escalates, volley to volley and then your friend, taking the ball and
spiking back, retaliates with something hurtful and mean, aiming
straight for your vulnerabilities, like, "Maybe if you weren't such
a nag, you might've gotten that promotion you were waiting for
and you could do what the heck you wanted for lunch!" Score,
both parties, both points! Food fest for the hungry energies and
an egoic, human experience served up with humble pie.

I am not saying, look for a demonic possession to recognize
dark energies. Just watch for uncomfortable, negative emotions
and there will be these fellows not far behind. When true communication is required, wait until you and the other party are in
a receptive, warmer mood, when anger is not flying, when seething hatred or self-hatred are not present. You seriously may have
to wait a week or two, but it is positively useless to engage in
genuine communication while compromised by intelligent dark
energy. In fact, as hard as this may be, there is a greater need for
forgiveness and forgetting when conversations with dark energies
present take place. You will know what I am talking about when
it happens. There will be a stinging comment left to flavor the
relationship. This is the attempt to open another doorway, to compromise another energy system, simply to feed, as all living beings
need to do. Try to see those hurtful comments spewed out in
hatred or resentment as weapons and not as a soul's genuine desire to connect with another divine soul.

I want to emphasize what it feels like to be alone with this
energy seething through your system. It colors your entire world,
making everything feel hopeless, ugly, negative, foul, generally
uncomfortable and dissatisfying. Ever have one of those days when
everything you try to type on your keyboard makes you feel you
are dyslexic? The more you try to finish the dang thing you are
writing, the more you become incapable of not only spelling, but
of manipulating your fingers at all in any coordinated fashion.
Then when you think you are almost done with the accursed task,

the computer crashes. You fume and steam and get generally pissy. You remember you forgot to press save. That's it! All your effort for nothing! Yes, you guessed right, our buddies; the leprechauns, the dybbukim, the sprites, whatever you want to call them are present and hungry. Your negative energy microbes or however you want to refer to them are simply doing what they do, feeding on the vibration of negative energy. The more they feed the more they feel compelled to multiply. Like with the bacteria, we simply have to create an environment that is not conducive to these beings.

CREATING A SPACE WHERE DARK ENERGIES CANNOT RESIDE

The space you must occupy is that of love. I know that may sound simple or childlike, but it is your *only*, I repeat, ***only*** protection against this dark energy. You cannot outsmart it or out yell it or anything else. Remember, it is accessing information that is primordial, every piece of information that ever existed. You have nothing up your sleeve better than that. Only love. That is the human gift.

So, in truly wanting to connect to your relationship gift, or even to your own highest self, put yourself in a space of love. I work with people everyday offering this same advice and many of them say to me, "How do I do that? I don't really have a lot of love in my life as an example." I suggest starting with something you really like, a cat, a piece of beautiful clothing, a wonderful dessert. Anything. One woman found what worked for her was the feeling she had when she truly forgave her son-in-law. That was the closest to love she had felt for a long time. That works. Then gradually grow from that thing to a person, maybe your mother at a special time in your life, a girlfriend who cared for you a lot, your favorite grocery clerk. Let that feeling of love grow, like a plant, water it and watch it grow. Finally, supplant the face of the person you need to connect with or are having a hard time loving over that feeling of love.

I know this is not an easy order. The first time I tried this, I thought it was an impossibility. I had a woman who was making my life miserable (that's how *I* saw it) and I couldn't seem to get her out from under my skin. I tried everything I could. Finally I came across this method in a book by the Buddhist Bhiksuni (nun), Thubten Chodron entitled *Open Heart, Clear Mind*. I gave it a try. I started with the memory of my mother caring for me as a sick infant (the epitome of unconditional love, I think) then went on to thoughts of my husband and sister and niece and pulled in all sorts of people and objects for about two weeks before I could finally pull her face in to this feeling of love. It must have worked, because even as I think if her now, years later, I really do well up with love for her.

DARK INTELLIGENCE AS TEACHERS

I do not want to paint of picture of these intelligent, but pesky, beings as evil. I do not believe they are evil, I believe that everything comes from the Creator of all, which I believe can only be based on the vibration of unconditional love. So why then would we have such bizarre, negative, annoying, even destructive beings that exist on our planet, as part of the human incarnation? I believe that they exist specifically as teachers for humans. That means that we need to see *them* as gifts also. I like to think that the bigger the dark energy that is trying to get into my energy space, the more I should feel privileged. I must be a strong enough student to elicit the biggest, "baddest" teacher. The harder the test, the more advanced the pupil. Of course, that's easy to say *now*, but while it is happening it feels like I'm wrestling with a rabid bear, losing and existing in a living hell. When I finally step out of an intense, negative learning experience, I can then see how it has assisted me in ways I have truly needed.

My experience is that we as humans, because of the free will factor, have a multitude of ways to learn and grow. I have boiled them down to two, the positive way and the negative way. I imagine on our journey we have this beautiful light shining ahead of us, leading us on, inspiring us, positively pulling us along to our goal. We get a nice way along the trip following the light and then want to rest. The journey is not that easy. So we sit for a while in a big comfortable chair, content with wherever we've gotten thus far, okay job, okay relationships, okay salary, living from weekend to weekend. Not bad, it sure could be worse. The light still beckons, but we have stopped paying attention, we are setting up camp here around this comfortable chair. The ego is careful and is pleased. The soul says, "I think not" and what enters into your life, stage left? Just what your soul ordered, you just don't remember. A negative teacher that starts poking you from under your chair, swatting your head, overturning the whole chair and destroying the camp if need be. While this is happening you are crying, "persecution", but the soul sees its destiny getting closer, sees the negative forces *pushing* you along to the goal that the positive light ahead wasn't effectively drawing you.

We have all experienced times when everything in life seemed to be gliding along, not really on cloud nine, but effortlessly, not much in the way of strife. Then all kinds of weird acts of nature and ill health and death and job loss occur. This would be our irritating friends, the dark energies, coupling with our inner desire to return to our divine nature, manifesting in our physical life. So they are not to be feared for who they are, only for our reaction to them.

If you have children or indulged yourself in the children's book series Harry Potter by J. K. Rowland, in the third book *Harry Potter and the Prisoner of Azkaban*, there appear creatures called *bogarts*. Part of the young wizard student's class assignment is to find these bogarts (in the closet) and meet them and disintegrate them. The class watches as each student opens the closet door and is greeted by some strange being. What the bogart does is form itself into the thing that each individual student is most afraid of in life. So the other students think it will be a breeze when it is their turn, they are not afraid of *that* bogart's shape at all. But when their turn arrives, they are frozen with fear, completely disarmed by their own personal bogart. This is what dark intelligence is like, exactly. They *will* hit you with your deepest fears, no doubt fears that need to be looked at and not run away from. Remember, they originate from the Divine. They are here to propel humans on their soul's journey. Maybe even they are those who do not evolve until we do not need them anymore in the Earth School. Give them the respect they deserve, do not take them lightly, they can destroy your life if you let them. They can also force you into your greatest strengths by illuminating your deepest weaknesses and ultimately act as the catalyst to find your highest self, that part of you required to face your greatest fears.

Imagine that you are very ill but continue eating only potato chips and bonbons for sustenance. Your physical self would not get much in the way of assistance to ward off this compromising illness. You know that you need to drink more clear liquids, sleep more, eat cleaner and lighter, stay home from work, take vitamins if necessary and arm your physical body with everything you have to fight off the germs or bacteria. This physical scenario is very similar to the energy-based one of being compromised by germs of the nonphysical nature also. Lighten your stress load, stay out of the company of those who ignite your worst emotions, do things for yourself that you enjoy and think of or be around those you genuinely love. Everything has its natural course, be it the flu or a bout with dark energies.

Listen to what others are *not* saying, and *how* they are saying it and remember that you may not be alone in your conversation. Make love your companion as often as possible, and you will not allow dark energy to control your words and actions. Remember, no matter what anyone says to you, how you respond is your choice. Like my mother always said, it takes two to tangle and if you choose not to tangle, your energy system remains intact, you remain immune from the negative effects of the darker energies. When you build your immunity by choice, those same dark and negative energies have strengthened you, pushed you along your soul's path. The idea for us is to care enough to work through our own various shortcomings and weaknesses so that we can connect with others, acknowledging and accepting their weaknesses along the way. The journey would be pretty lonesome if we all had to go it alone.

6 How Relationships Help us Grow

The Gift

I placed it in my carrying basket
and slung it over my handlebars
and pedaled myself purposefully down the dirt track.
I slowed down to admire the yellow and red markings
that painted the turtle that soaked up the sun,
just at the base of those lacy white flowers made from a queen.
I detoured into the meadow to lay on the grasses,
the stems tickling my bare legs — looking up through
sky blue chicory, golden rod and the black eyes of Susan.
Angel wings flew gracefully across the sky in wisps of delight.
A delicate web caught my attention and I marveled at the
construction and loveliness of the spider's pantry.
Oh, yes. I have something to deliver.
Back on my old blue bike with the wire basket and leaky tire

Moving solidly along the track, through the big pot hole,
mud splattered, legs getting sore, up the steep hill,
gliding freely down the other side.
The German shepard saw me before I came out of my day dream
and chased and barked and showed those slobbery yellow teeth.
I pushed hard and lifted myself off the seat to get more power to my legs,
to fly, to get away, my heart in a frenzy to match the receding sound
of the barking dog, I continue on.
I arrive here, tired, muddy, wet from the rain that has begun to fall
gently from an unconcerned sky
I drop my bike beside the path that leads up to the door of a cozy cottage
with yellow light from the windows warming the near dark garden.
I pause and reach into my basket, grasp what I have brought
and by the filtered light of the house, I examine it.
A stone.
On one side it is smooth and my fingers naturally glide over the face,
reveling in its flawless, smooth, perfect beauty.
As the light sparkles off the bluish, purple pink colors, I believe for a moment,
I can see the splendor of the universe in its face.
Just then I feel the rough, unpolished and raw facets of the stone.
The earthy shades of brown and tan intertwine and root the purple
and blue to earth.
I knock on the door and you open it, a soft smile of anticipation
and friendship on your face.
I smile back and take your hand and gently, carefully, place the stone
in your palm, curl your fingers over it, squeeze lightly
and go back
to my blue bike, to the dirt track, to the night sky.

-Jan Hutslar (2003)

That poem was written as a response to me by my sister, and I thought it was a perfect way to begin this chapter. The reason is that my whole premise for writing this book is that relationships are gifts and once we see what they are offering, and can accept it, that is when our own healing takes place. The rock in the poem represents her, my sister, to me. The polished part of the rock is her divine self, a sum of all that is beautiful that exists in the universe. The raw, unpolished part represents the part she is still working on, and the part that may occasionally rub others wrong. But the total of all parts is who she is and if I don't accept her that way, if I wait for the other side to become polished by the winds and the rain, I may miss a very beautiful relationship.

As I mentioned in the first chapter, I feel very strongly that each relationship has a purpose. Some are to support us in this life, others to challenge us. Some show up for a short time to provide the catalyst to push us through something, sometimes the hard way, and others are on this journey with us for the duration. Some relationships are there to provide inspiration and guidance in a positive way. Others are there to provide a negative example for us. I believe that we all have agreements we have made about what we are going to do in this life. I think we do end up doing those things, but not always as the positive embodiment of the promises we made. Oftentimes we do it by becoming the negative example, not necessarily out of conscious choices, but fulfilling our contract nonetheless. It seems to me (a positively poled person) that it would be a lot more fun and life would be more enjoyable if we chose the positive way of living out what we came here to do. But often, that isn't the case. Let me give you a few examples.

If you came here to teach the lesson of accepting personal responsibility for one's own life and actions, you could be the example of that. You could embody the very essence of responsibility for both your actions and your words. You would not carry victim energy or blame others for your rotten situation. You would learn how to see the effects of your decisions and accept and alter them as needed. Your life would be an example, without teaching anything, of what you came here to do. That's one way. The other, what I call the lesser-self way, but which still fulfills your contract nonetheless, would be to show others what it is like to *not* accept responsibility for anything that happens to you in your life. You would blame your parents, your sister, your spouse and your children all for making your life miserable. Every action would be a result of someone else's bad decisions, as you see it. Or there's always God to blame too, when everyone else has left your life. God is punishing you, creating the worst situation possible for you, and if it weren't for that, you'd be doing some fabulous this or that. Living life in this way you would also present an example of learning personal responsibility, but just the backwards way, as I call it. People who experience you in their lives see the repeated motif and the endless cycle, as nothing changes. They think to themselves, "Wow, I don't think I want to be like that, because then when I am very old, I would have done nothing myself except blame others for an unfulfilled life. Hmm, think I'll try something else." And so you have essentially saved them years of learning things the way you did; the hard way. You see, either way, you have done what you came here to do.

Now, we as participants in this game of life will either play out one role or another. We will be thrown into a cast of people who either rub us the wrong way, or are shining examples of greatness or a mix of both. What I want to explore in depth is why are these characters who rub us the wrong way in our lives? You know my belief. It is for a reason. That reason is ultimately growth, for us and for them. I have heard people explain relationships saying, "I helped him a whole lot, but never got anything out of that relationship." That is nothing more than a one-sided understanding of the relationship. You may *feel* all you did was help him, but realize it or not, you got something more. You may have gotten the message that you, or he, got tired of you helping him. Maybe he got tired of feeling inadequate and needing fixing, thus giving honor and value to himself. Maybe you got tired of giving without reciprocation, which causes resentment, so to cease doing so would give value to you also. It is a two-way street. No relationship (that I have come across) is for one person only, to the sacrifice of the other.

Let's look at some specific types of relationships.

PARENT/CHILD RELATIONSHIPS

Sometimes looking at our own issues is the hardest thing. Why can we see others' so plainly, but ours elude us? Look to where your children are pointing their blunt fingers. The answer could be very close. When they light up issues for you about your own inadequacy or feelings of being powerless, for example, try to measure your response on a scale of 0-10. Ten being red-hot, all-alert, time to pay attention, seriously intense emotion, zero being no emotional response whatsoever. If you are registering anywhere near an eight, take heed, these children are your gifts. They are lighting up or pushing the buttons that open the door to self-awareness and then healing. Remember, we don't have control over others, but only over our responses to them. You might be compelled to say, "They did this or that to me and I can't help how angry I am." Or, "They *made* me react like this." They only presented an obstacle. Interestingly, as Elaine Pagels points out in *The Origins of Satan,* the Greek word *diabolos*, translated as *devil* in English, simply means "one who throws something across one's path," and the root term of the word *Satan* in Hebrew means "one who opposes, obstructs or acts as adversary." Many times the parents are being the diabolos and other times the children are. This does not mean either is being evil, or devilish, but genuinely providing the perfect obstacle for the perfect growth. Both are expressions of higher love for each other. You may now be thinking, this woman obviously does not have a teenager. First, I would like to point out that I did, and when I did I was unable to see that relationship in the terms I am trying to teach now. Every relationship has a purpose and the relationship with my own teen-ager helped plant the seeds for this book years later. The sooner we embrace the possibility of a purpose, the sooner we can have a peaceful, loving relationship. As long as we are not heeding the messages our children came to deliver, they will find louder and more annoying ways to deliver their messages. It is often the chil-dren who give us the most grief, so to speak. They are the ones with which our souls have a contract of challenge and they en-courage us to learn and grow. Whereas those children who are dolls may be there for much needed support, but are not showing up in the capacity of challengers (at least not at the moment, they may engage that role later in life).

LEVELS OF EXPRESSION

Before we move on to the other types of relationships, let me introduce another concept that helps understanding, from the perspective of the teacher and the student (whoever is playing which role). There are three levels of expressing who we are, uniquely. While I have simplified them into just three, there are infinite shades of gray along the scale from one to another. There is the *lowest,* the *median* and the *highest expression* of who we can be in this life. You cannot go through the experience of raising young teens without discovering where along the spectrum you express yourself. The lowest expression of the self is just that, given any situation, one reacts without conscious thought or without curbing the bruised ego and what results is the lowest we have to offer as humans. The median is a middle choice. It would contain elements of self-control but with limits and attempts to honor and understand, again with limits. The highest is just what it sounds like. It is the closest to our most divine nature that we can hope to express while in a human body. It would be allowing the soul to connect with the other person's soul and bypass the emotional drama of the egos involved. It would include understanding or attempting understanding even when the other party is not encouraging an honoring communication.

I am not here to say you have to live the highest expression of who you are, but only that your relationship gifts will undoubtedly point it out to you, and probably not so kindly, if it is anything other than the highest. Once again, we see the gift in action, pushing us to our potential if we can just hear what is not being said, understand what is not being communicated, and respond in a way that is healing for us as well as for them. How do we do this?

I have a family I work with in California. I worked first with their eight-year-old son, his mother and then his father. The son was a difficult child, and they had been through counseling together and individually, tried child-psychiatrist prescribed drugs, more counseling, threats, drugs and more counseling. After I worked with him his attitude greatly improved, although he was still a live wire, and still pushed his parents to their limits, certainly before they were ready for the challenge. After a lot of soul searching, now coming from the place of seeing his issues as reflections of what both parents needed to understand or overcome, they took him off his medication, reduced therapy and talked with him. They realized he needed to be a part of creating his own life. The rules they created as parents were just things Travis simply loved to break. They both realized after working together in our sessions that they had issues of power. Travis' father didn't feel he had enough, subconsciously, and his mother felt she was too domineering, making everyone succumb to her wishes and demands. She knew that this was in response to her own need to control her world, not trusting that others would do it right. So here was young Travis, saying, "Wanna look at stuff now?" He did not seem to give them any choices other than adoption or suicide (which they probably contemplated late at night!).

They came up with what I thought was an excellent solution. They decided to let him make his own rules. He could go to bed when he wanted, get up when he wanted, do his chores and homework when he chose. As long as he knew that the consequences were his. So if he did not get his homework done, it would be him getting punished by the teacher, if he did not get enough sleep, it would be him who suffered the next day in school. He still had chores in the family to do, but it was his choice when and how he could do them. It was taking a big risk, but both parents talked about it and felt good about the option.

I talked to them several weeks into the project and everyone seemed to be doing incredibly well. Mom was letting go of the feeling that her way was the only way. Dad was feeling better about Travis than he ever had. He wasn't making him feel powerless every time he defied his authority, and Travis was truly living up to being trusted. He was even doing more than he was asked, helping his younger brother, feeling big and wanting to help others. How creative! What a true healing experience for everyone.

I know two families who, through divorce, shared one child. At the ripe young age of 13, she began to give both sets of parents a difficult time. When she was with her mother, she felt like she could not be herself. She felt dishonored and trapped in a lifestyle that she abhorred. When she was with her father, she felt like she could never live up to his expectations. One life was below her, she felt, the other was unattainable. She was not thriving in either family. What was finally decided after sending her back and forth for a year and a half was to allow her to be truly who she was in her *own* environment. The parents found a live-in school that was based on the concept of being self-sufficient. They were taught how to cook, garden, repair things, clean and take care of themselves in most every respect. Essentially, it was the young people who ran the school. They did not have a crew of cooks or groundskeepers. Students with these interests could elect to do these as their chores and in doing so helped pay their own way. It was a drastic solution, no doubt, but creative, when seemingly all else failed. Here the idea was to allow their daughter to flower in a way that was not limiting or impossible. At the same time, it offered a solution to the parents who were feeling inadequate in every natural thing they did. For both, they learned something invaluable, the father to relinquish control and trust his daughter, for the mother, that her life-style wasn't bad, it just could not be forced upon another, even if it is your own offspring. In theory, both families learned lessons of honoring and valuing each individual, regardless of who felt who should be what. Even though it was a heartfelt response to a teenager's cry, it wasn't until several years later and many difficult experiences that this family could find genuine joy and companionship with each other. The key was, they never stopped trying to connect and find the plug that worked.

What I tell my clients when we are doing healing work related to their childhood and they find that they are still carrying issues about their parents is that your parents are people who are just a little bit older than you. Quite often we hold these impossible demands and unrealistic images of our parents. They didn't love me enough. They didn't guide me. They didn't accept me. They never cared about what I did. They loved my sister more, and so on. Most of these complaints reflect back upon each of us and highlight our own specific missing pieces. My theory is that we are all complete individuals, we just don't know it. We are constantly looking for the missing piece, but we can't get it from someone else or *they* would then have a missing piece. So we have to find it within ourselves.

In her book *Sacred Contracts*, Carolyn Myss analyzes the symbolism in the movie *The Wizard of Oz* using a beautiful example of the cowardly lion. He was looking for his missing piece (in fact, in Dorothy's dream, it was actually her own missing pieces represented by the lion, the scarecrow and the rest of the characters). The lion was told he had to perform an act of courage (bring-

ing back the broom of the Wicked Witch of the West) before the
wizard would grant him his request of courage. He had to discover for himself that a courageous heart was in him all along.

In each of your children, as in each of us, is something they
have come here to locate. We have what some people call core
issues, and we have missing pieces. That does not mean that we
are defective or not whole, not at all. We just don't embody our
completeness yet. We have to *re-remember* where the pieces are.
For example, some people have what I call heart problems, but
this is not about the functioning of the physical heart (although it
can eventually transmit its energetic resonances to the physical
body). It is about the perceived ability to give or receive love.
They seem to search their entire life for that special person who
will complete them, give them the love they so desire or find the
grateful receiver of all their heart's love. The story that I have seen
played out again and again with this particular vibration of in-
completeness is that the person they finally attract into their lives
is the opposite of who their minds wanted, but instead is someone who responded perfectly to the energetic pattern they had
broadcast at a level much deeper than the mental. The mates they
end up with are ones who either are unable to love (responding to
the pure vibration of being unlovable) or are cold and aloof (responding to that clean message of being unable to give love). Either way, what it feels like is persecution of the most severe type.
The thing we most want is denied us. I like to look at it like this,
if we already *had* something that we came here specifically to
embody completely, would we bother to look for it?

Some people might say, why don't we know we are complete
to start with? Save that question for your Maker some day and get
back to me, okay?

Back to parents, what you came here to re-remember is probably not the same thing that your daughter or son came here to
do. I was talking with a woman just the other day and she said, "I
just don't understand my son. He's so afraid. He's afraid to talk to

me. He's afraid of getting into his feelings. But for crying out loud, I'm his mother! Why should he be afraid?" I had to remind her that she is a very courageous person by nature and that even though she doesn't have any fears doesn't mean that others don't. Courage is part of his journey. Maybe that's why they were together, she could help him learn courage and he could help her learn compassion and balance. Living up to our highest self is the perfect solution, but so often we don't quite measure up to what we conceive of, in theory, as our highest self. Putting it into practice is more difficult to be sure.

Let's look at a common everyday occurrence that can be dealt with in one of our three ways of expressions. Imagine that there is a huge expectation that you anticipate happening, be it a job promotion or a nomination as a class officer in school. You feel you deserve it because you have worked very hard for it. But the ultimate day comes and in fact, someone else is chosen. Let's look first at someone living in their *lowest* expression. This does not mean this is *who* they are, it just means this is how they have chosen (consciously or unconsciously) to express themselves in this situation at this time. Through the lowest expression of ourselves, the response is going to be something like this: bitter resentment, anger and a vengeful desire to get back at someone, either the one who made the decision, or the one who received the promotion or nomination. The *median* expression person would not be as emotionally violent, or blame anyone else, but may see this as a personal sign from above, and become the victim, "Poor me, nothing ever comes my way, no matter how hard I work for it. Oh well, nothing I can do, I am powerless, I guess." And finally, someone representing their *highest* expression will congratulate the recipient of the position they themselves worked so hard for and will either offer their services to support this new position, or move on to another position for which they are possibly more suited. Often we pursue positions out of prestige and not out of our heart's desire, so having our goals redirected for us often sends us in a better direction in the long run. Much of our own karma, or past experiences, may dictate where we land in this life, but having control over our responses is our own, right now. Also, watching others expressing themselves in a lower mode does not make you better, hopefully it just makes you more understanding, as we have all responded as our lowest self at some time.

I truly don't believe there can be any victims in this world if we actually are co-creators of our own lives. Did we not place our teachers in strategic places along the road before we came into this life for perfect learning experiences? Did we not choose someone we loved and were related to (who we could not run away from) to help us? Who else would help us in such a painful or uncomfortable way? Only those who really love us. Sometimes I think that the ones in our lives who are the biggest thorns in our sides are those who we have loved the most in our past, because everyone else would give up and say, "Forget it, lady!" I get a kick out of imagining what crazy things we are doing before we come down here onto Earth. I can just see us sitting around saying, "Okay, I'm going to need someone to help me get over my overly strong sense of ego if I am ever to embody my whole spiritual self, but who? Who is strong enough? *You*? Oh, okay. Yeah, I can do that." Then my wise counselor says, "Are you sure you want Brutus Gargantuan? Once you get down there you will forget you picked him." I say, "Naw, I can do this (of course, I am surrounded by love and wisdom and support at the time) I've got to do it, let's get on with it. Bring it on!" Later, when Brutus Gargantuan enters my life of course I'll scream, "PERSECUTION!!!! Why would the gods punish me so?"

Many times those closest to us, our parents or children, will offer us the greatest learning experience if only we can see beyond the emotions we are feeling, step into a neutral zone and evaluate the whats and hows. I work with a woman who has been working through the same issue of acceptance from her mother for over 50 years. She is waiting to feel good about herself only after her mother treats her like a beautiful, worthy human being. That does not seem forthcoming given their dynamic. The conflict and negativity just grow stronger and more intense with each year, but the daughter is stubbornly caught in the mind-set that this acceptance is what she needs to feel worthy. In the meantime, she can't get or keep a job, has been divorced four times, kicked out of homes and had her car repossessed. My thought is, she might try another game plan. You know the definition of insanity, right? Doing the same thing again and again while expecting different results. This mother is vigilantly teaching her daughter, quite unknowingly, that her own self-worth does not come from anyone outside one's own self. She is as stubbornly sticking to her agreement to teach this lesson as her daughter is in rebelling against learning it.

Several years ago one of my sisters got married. It was her second marriage and one we were all pleased to see take place, so my entire clan decided to attend the wedding. I think it was because we all intuitively knew (at our age) that the next opportunity for a family gathering of this size would be someone's funeral. So here was a lovely opportunity for every living Hutslar, and a few on my mother's side thrown in, to get together for a joyous occasion. At first we were all excited, but as the date grew nearer, everyone started having their own reactions, physical and emotional, about seeing all the people and issues (mostly the issues they represented) they thought they had left behind. I started talking with each of my siblings individually and realized each one was still holding on to some unresolved thing or another. One sister still felt that our parents hadn't ever given her the amount and quality of love she really needed, and seeing them again lit up that deficit. One sister was coming only because everyone else was and didn't want to be left out, but in actuality the sister getting married lit up her own feelings of jealousy and rivalry. We are talking about grown adults, not teenagers. Two brothers on my father's side were still carrying issues of authority and acceptance that needed to be let go of from 1964.

My suggestion is get the issues out and dealt with as young as possible so you're not still grappling with them forever. Maybe this isn't even possible, but if we could open the door to understanding, couldn't it help us to at least be able to recognize what is ours and what is not and how to go about finding and filling those needs? We could see our children as the gifts they were meant to be and uncover this mysterious lesson they come to teach and be grateful instead of resentful. We could appreciate the differences in our parents and us because those very differences are what light up our learning. Instead of judging, us against them, our way versus their way, win/lose, we could see why *we* (the important pronoun) chose them as our parents or as our children. We would be taking responsibility for something that traditionally has not been thought possible, our own lives. Point the finger back on the finger pointer. It's not your mother who ruined your life, it is your mother who is diligently loving your soul so much that she will never renege on her agreement to challenge you in a way that could help your soul along its journey immeasurably!

PARTNERS

This is probably my favorite topic. I love being in love, I love loving and being committed to my life partner, my husband who is also my best friend. I have been known to fix people up for the purpose of a long-term relationship, not just a passing fling, because I have found so much happiness in having a partner with whom to share life. That being said, I am convinced that your partner is almost always the one in your life prepared to create the *hardest* challenges for you. That person is perhaps the closest, living together day in and day out, sharing toothpaste (the common denominator for living together these days), and without a doubt lighting up most of your core issues. This does not mean that your partner is someone of the opposite sex to whom you are committed. It could very well be the person you have chosen to accompany you in this life. It could be your mother, or aunt or niece or sister or friend or lover. That person who plays the dominant role in your daily life is who we will refer to as your partner. I also did not say that you had to have *chosen* them consciously. You may think that you did not, that you are thrown together because of circumstances, but invariably, on some level, I believe you chose each other.

Currently divorce in this country hits two out of three marriages. This statistic tells me that there must be some serious challenging going on. One way to deal with issues we are not ready to look at or that are presented in a package we are not ready to open is to leave that particular gift behind. Trust me, I am not saying that divorce is not a positive thing in many cases. I am just saying it shows how often we engage in a learning experience that either we get, and move through or, more often, feel unprepared to meet the challenge offered by that relationship and choose to remove ourselves.

Let's look at some core issues. What about trust? That is a core issue and I see this every day in the work I do with clients. I also find that if one of my clients is carrying the vibration of betrayal, as I like to word it, they will draw, guess who? Those who are untrustworthy and can fulfill their unconscious desire to be betrayed. Relationship after relationship ends in the same way. I worked with a woman last year who had been married three times where the first two marriages ended in divorce because her husbands were having affairs with other women. She always had many descriptive words for these bum ex-husbands of hers, promising that if she ever married again she would not allow that to happen again. For her, it was the most sinful of all things, it was a personal insult to her, to her love and her femininity. Of course, if you believe that is the biggest issue of all in a marriage, well, then it will be. It's *your* life! Finally, after a year and a half into the third marriage, she found out her new husband was seeing many other women, most of whom were his students. At this point, instead of screaming divorce, she came to see me and admitted that she was beginning to think it was her, and not them. She was attracting a certain type of man, but she didn't know why and it really hurt. This is where your own healing begins. When you take that first step in the AA 12-step program and stand up and say, I am so and so and I am attracting a certain kind of person again and again and I am sick of it!

How do you stop attracting a person who betrays? Well, you stop carrying the vibration of betrayal. How do you do that? First you identify that that is what it is. Then you must decide if you really want to let go of it or not. While working together, I often ask my clients, "Do you really want to let go of whatever the core issue is?" You should hear the hesitation, the squeaky voices, the contrived confidence. It brings you to the next step. If I am not yet willing or ready to let this go, why am I holding on to it? Does it provide a necessary handicap? Is it a way to gain attention or sympathy? Do I define myself as this thing, as dysfunctional as it is, and without it would I lose my identity? You see the complexity here? So before you can say, "Be gone with you, you evil force, *betrayal*," you have to determine if any of your subtle bodies are ready to pay attention and obey. So you may need to do quite a bit of work determining who you will be without this ever present shadow keeping you partially in the dark at all times. Are you really ready to shine all of your light, to stick out, to have others pay attention to you because of your brightness? Before we go on to the next step, let's look at partners some more.

Let's say you have issues of powerlessness. If you resonate with being powerless, you will most likely attract someone who has issues of control. Let me interject here, it is only after intense internal reflection that one admits they have issues with power. What I have witnessed is that those with the biggest issues of control or lack of feeling genuinely powerful are the very ones who try to control every little thing. You may know someone like this who tries to control everything in their work environment down to the timing of when each employee takes lunch and potty breaks. It appears to the rest of the world that they have been allocated an *overdose* of power. Energetically they are trying to make up for that missing piece we spoke of earlier.

Back to our couple finding their perfect match while carrying the vibration of powerlessness. Let's say Stan is our willing example of a man with internal feelings of lack of control in the world around him. He meets and connects up with Janice who has an obsession with control. She is fanatical about being in control of every event in her life and anyone around her. Stan enters into the lesson. First, he feels off the hook in having to make any decisions for awhile, decisions that only show him how impotent he feels, by joining forces with Janice who will gladly do everything for him. But what is control except another face of powerlessness? If you completely trust that the Universe is unfolding exactly as it was meant to, do you really need to be in control of anything? Participating, cooperating, living up to your end of your agreements certainly, but controlling? What do we really have control over anyway?

Shortly, Stan realizes that not a day goes by that Janice doesn't shove in his face (or so it appears to Stan) his own issues of lack of power. If she makes all the decisions, cares for the finances under the strictest regime, dictates his world, sooner or later Stan's suppressed internal voice will make its debut. One way of looking at Janice's role is to see her as a spring board. Some may feel she is being restrictive and oppressive, but maybe that is exactly what Stan needs. Janice provides the catalyst to *force* Stan to claim what is his and also at the same time provide the opportunity for Janice to let go of some of the jurisdiction over which she so dearly resides. She gets the chance, in the name of a loving relationship, to trust someone and allow herself to be taken care of. Maybe the universe won't end if she isn't taking care of every little detail from morning 'till night. There will be times you love this person dearly, are glad and secure that they are dealing with life issues you cannot face. And there will be other times you despise the day they were born. They will *make* you feel (remember, you are responding, they are not actually *making* you) like an insignificant protozoan.

How do you determine what is the life issue your present relationship gift is helping you through? That is a very good question. You may be together for 12 or 42 years before you ever understand why you are in the relationship. Sometimes I think people choose each other because they don't want to look at their own stuff this time around, but it seems that inevitably it does surface. I guess the way you can evaluate your partner, or any relationship, is ask this question, *"Who do they force me to be?"* Once again I don't mean that they physically force you, I mean that your response forces a set of circumstances that enact your karmic baggage. Do they challenge every belief you have, forcing you to look at your core beliefs, trashing the ones that are hollow and creating the urgency to embody those you truly believe? Or do they break you down into being their clone? Do they force you to own your own authenticity by handing you a pre-prepared solution to every one of life's problems, even though they may not be the solution you would choose on your own? Do they belittle you when you try to grow or ask you to do things they believe are above you, forcing you to stand up and be the intelligent capable person you were meant to be? Do they try to fix you or make your life better, making you finally look at your life and ask, "What was so wrong with me that I should need so much fixing?" Or do they leave you feeling you could not exist without their help? Do you see the theme? Partners challenge. They are the diabolos or rocks in your path that force you to make choices about moving and growing. Are you going to fight it? Are you going to go around it? Are you going to stand there and cry? Are you going to climb over it? No one is going to come and remove your rock. You can say, I quit, and go back to another path, but eventually you will meet up with Mr. or Ms. Diabolos again. The other day I was walking past a city park and saw a group of kids playing tag. One boy began chasing another very fast and both were running hard. Finally, when the boy being chased got tagged, he said, "I don't want to play this game anymore." That is one response. Maybe it is even the appropriate one if we do not feel we are ready on some level, or if we are in our comfortable chair phase of life.

Another way of answering the 'who does this person force me to be' question is to see how you are reacting to them. Maybe you are not yet in the healing phase and cannot see the positive that can come from the abuse or negativity. You then need to see how they make you feel about yourself. Do they make you feel insignificant? Worthless? Unlovable? Incapable? Ashamed? Guilty? If they elicit emotional responses from you with these vibrations attached to them, you can be sure that some of your baggage is in there. Remember the scale of emotional response from 0-10? If they *make* you feel guilty, you must look at your own stuff and ask, "What is it about me they are accessing, that they could light this up?" You know the old saying, if the shoe fits, wear it? The corollary is, if it doesn't, then don't. But if it feels emotional, try to look inward, don't turn your emotionally ignited ego back on your partner. Try to see what you yourself feel guilty about and make the decision to deal with that. That means whatever that means. I am not naïve enough to think that I can say, "If you feel guilty, then stop it and go on with your life." I was reading a book the other day, and in it the author gives suggestions for dealing with certain things. He says essentially that, if you find yourself feeling insecure about something, stop feeling insecure and go on to number two. Number two was more of the same. Anyway, the issues are yours, not your partner's. They are only holding a flashlight as you work on the engine of your life. Don't hit the flashlight holder for showing you that you need an engine overhaul!

On the other hand, they may be *making* you feel powerful and wonderful things. This could be to light up issues of lack of value, worthless or dishonored, or it may be to provide the positive example of someone who lives their truths, and teaches by living. This is great, but most relationships I deal with are not wholly positive or wholly negative, they are a unique combination of both, depending upon the individuals.

You could have a partner who is a control freak, for sure, but that does not necessarily mean you have issues with power. You may not respond to their controlling behavior at all, and go along with your life taking the control you desire and leaving your partner to deal with their own issues of control. The way you determine what is yours is by the amount of emotional response you find yourself having to your partner's actions or words. Here we need to distinguish between your emotions and theirs. Yes, it's true, others can get you all embroiled in their emotionalism. Remember the feeling communicators? I remember once in high school I was taking square dance lessons with the son of a friend of my parents. We were not romantically involved, we were just borrowing each other to learn how to square dance. I didn't know anything about him, other than his part in dancing. Then one evening on the way home he chose to confide in me things about his private life and his use of drugs and I can't remember what else. But at 16 years old, I know it shocked me, which is probably what he had meant to do. I went home and went to my room and sat on my bed and cried, thinking, what a horrible thing. It felt really creepy. I could feel myself getting sucked into his drama, but then after about 10 minutes, I stopped crying and thought, "Why am I crying? I don't even *know* this guy," and then relaxedly went about my business. Differentiating between what belongs to us and what belongs to others lightens the emotional load we need to carry.

There are also those who are emotionally abusive and manipulative. They use emotions like anger or guilt to get what they want and to get others to do things without their consent, and subsequently, become dishonoring and using. These can be very powerful emotions, and when you are in the presence of anger especially, it is really hard to not feel it and respond by either recoiling or retaliating. So it is best to be in an emotionally neutral space before you determine what is really your garbage and what is not. One woman I know who obviously does not have guilt as one of her issues, says that her mother would openly use guilt to get her six children to do what she wanted them to do. Some would succumb, but this daughter would look her mom in the face and say, "I ain't packin' my bags, I'm not goin' on any guilt trip, thanks!" This is how you know it is not your stuff, there is no real emotional response to a strong stimulus. Another way you can double-check that you are on the right track in locating your issues is when you are alone and thinking about a conversation you had with your partner that lit you up big time. What part of the conversation still bugs you? What part hurt you the most? Look there. And don't kid yourself, it is all about you right now, be brutally honest.

Then there are those who are numb. That means they don't feel *anything*. I don't suspect I will be getting a lot of readers like that, but you may be in a partnership with someone who is. They have mastered the art of dulling the senses as a way of coping, either through medication, alcohol, continuous illnesses or simply emotionally tuning out. These people have serious difficulty facing some of the things they put in their paths this life. That is okay. Life can be pretty hard and who are we to say what others are capable of? Especially if they don't believe they are capable themselves. Anyway, it is not your job to get these people to un-numb, or maybe it is, I guess that depends on what you signed up for. What I meant to say was, they have to be ready and willing to turn their feelers back on, you cannot hypersensitize them by pushing large volumes of strong emotion on them to get *some* response.

I think we've about covered most of the ways we can avoid and respond and magnetize and heal and learn. I want to continue on with this thought about what to do now that we have uncovered a core issue and truly want to deal with it. Let's imagine that this thing, this emotion or issue or whatever we want to call it, resides in a particular place in us. That place has a door to it. Sometimes we open it, (or rather it is kicked open for us) and other times we keep it shut and locked. My suggestion is to locate this place, your heart, your stomach, your head, your psychic self, wherever, and open the door, better yet, take the door off. And, this is the really hard part, go into the room.

Say, for example, at the core of you, you believe that you are *unlovable*. Consciously or not, you are led to believe that it must be there due to all the emotional responses about it. You feel not wholly ever loved by your parents, not unconditionally loved by your God, not loved always by your mate and not loved by yourself. You can say these words and they sting a little, but undoubtedly, you have ways to make up for these feelings. You have your work, you fling yourself completely into it. You have your food, it always loves you. You have your obsessions, whatever. Step away from all those things and only enter into the room that holds this feeling that you are unlovable. Face it. Ask where it came from, you may have been born with it in this life, but you were not created with this misinformation by the Divine. So you must have acquired it somewhere. Maybe it won't speak to you. Maybe you have pretended it wasn't there for so long that it seems invisible. Now you have to be creative. You may need to speak to it, have a decent conversation, without blaming or deriding. You may need to be grateful. Perhaps it has played a part in who you are now, and that isn't that bad, remember? This may take minutes or hours or months. The process is in facing it. The more you face it, the more others will inherently feel this vibration at the surface of your energy system and unfortunately, respond likewise. I wish I could say they will lay off until you've figured it out, but the truth is quite to the contrary. Every little thing will exacerbate this sting-ing, open wound. Know that it is for your highest good, really (well, I always tell myself that, and anyway, what choice do you have?).

Speaking of partners, I have described to my husband the visual image I have of how he gets me to look at my own issues is to grab hold of me and force me over to a closet door that holds my deepest fear, throw open the door, toss me in and *lock* the door behind me! That's the way it *feels* at the time. I don't think he is very patient once he discovers something that needs atten-tion that I am ignoring, for any reason whatsoever. After 20-some years together, I feel like I am braver and stronger and have faced more of my closet monsters than I would have without his prompt-ing. I also know that when the others arrive, he will be there to locate the entrance to each personal closet-monster door. Part of his personal gift is the uncanny ability to perceive another's shadow area. That is usually where the things we don't want to look at reside.

So here you are, in the closet with your fear. Maybe your issue *is* fear. It won't be easy. In fact, there is a very good reason you haven't faced it before, it is terrifying. Let me add something here I have found while locating many past-life stories to help heal the individual of today. That is that we don't take on a belief for *no* reason. There is always a *very* good reason at the time that we acquire a new belief about ourselves or the world around us. It is usually for survival purposes or to make sense of something that we could not possibly understand any other way. For example, if you are almost beaten to death by a violent mate for physically acting upon the love of your heart, you may carry some serious issues about what you have to sacrifice for a true love. That is stored there for a seriously important reason, *to keep you alive*!!! So do not underestimate the strength of these beliefs about the self that you are confronting in your closets.

The special gift of the partner is that they are there every day with us. We may want to say, "I don't want to play this game anymore", or "That emotional reaction I had last night when you were asking about why I gave up my dream to be a pianist was nothing, really." They are still there, holding the place on the game board for us. Saying, here's what comes next, it's *your* turn. You may run away and leave that game, but by some uncanny twist of fate you land right smack on the same square in a similar game played somewhere else. Now when you really do face your fear, heal your wound, whatever you want to call it, you may seriously be ready to move on. If your mate is not ready or willing to continue on to a more advanced game board, your soul will continue with or without them. I know a woman who was married for about 14 years and then was diagnosed with cancer. She went through a difficult bout with her health and subsequently changed everything about her previous life. She was more alive than she'd ever been, even though so close to death. Her husband put his foot down, he said, "I cannot change like that." He had not had a catastrophe to propel him. She tried and tried to get him to grow with her, but finally he said, "You are no longer the woman I married and I did not want these deep challenges, I don't want to be married to you anymore." He had every right to do that. And she had every right to move on, which is what she did.

That is the other side of the coin I have yet to mention. You will be lighting up the unhealed issues of your partner at the same time they are lighting up yours. Oh, doesn't that make things interesting? What belongs to whom? That is why it is important to own what is yours and take responsibility, and to allow what is not to exist. It may be for the greater purpose of helping to heal the one you love. Those with the same issues will either find it easier or impossible. I haven't figured that out yet. Sometimes mates with the same issues tend to both want to leave the closet door locked, because it represents the same scary thing for both of them. Other times, they can see their mate as a mirror, reflecting the traits they dislike most in themselves.

The most important thing to bear in mind through your whole mate-as-gift-and-being-shoved-in-the-closet thing, is this, if you make love your assistant, the whole process will go thousands of degrees more smoothly. I often see that this is the problem, the inability to love, oneself or others or both. With self-hate as your assistant, everything becomes more difficult. But then, well, that's the course load you signed up for, so I guess you must have had a reason. Sometimes the things we go through are for the purpose of experience. As my husband is so fond of saying, "If my soul had wanted a *soulful* experience it would've stayed where it was, but it wanted a *human* experience, that's why I'm a human!" I believe we are souls having a human experience, not humans having an occasional soulful experience. There is a subtle difference in our beliefs.

So keep in mind, your partners are here to challenge you in ways you could not do alone. The process of going through the most difficult and challenging issues and fears of your life truly do make for the material that bonds. This is another reason why partners are not only the most challenging, potentially, they can be the most rewarding. When you come out of the room you feared and you have made restitution, there is your partner waiting outside the door, guarding it for you. You never forget that. Even if it feels at the time like they are holding the door shut, afterwards, you see that their love kept them monitoring the door the whole time. I mean their soul's love for you, though you may not consciously see or feel their love outwardly. Know that for as difficult as they can be in your life, they have that much potential love for you.

COWORKERS

Years ago I worked in a traditional office setting that was really quite pleasant. I had a position as a manager and usually had the power to change things that seemed ineffective or that exhibited lack of integrity. I was well respected and truly enjoyed my coworkers. Well, all except one. This one woman drove me insane. I had to interact with her because of our respective jobs, but avoided her whenever I could. I tried being nice to her. I tried avoiding her. I tried complimenting her. I just found that I loathed being in her presence. This went on for seven years. How could I have been so slow? We all have our own process, remember that. Finally, I woke up enough to let my inner guidance help me look at this relationship in a different way. I had to look at her and ask myself this question, *"What do I dislike about her the most?"* Okay, I thought, that seemed easy enough, but it turned out to be more difficult than I expected. I found myself saying, *"everything."* After closer scrutiny, I found that wasn't exactly the truth. She really did have some redeeming characteristics, I was just blinded to them because of my own intolerances. I finally realized that the one thing I disliked about her the most was that she made me feel bad about myself. Why? Well, she always seemed to get me to gossip about our other coworkers, people about whom I was keeper of private information because of my position in the company. I really hated that about myself. No matter how much resolve I had, after being in her office for five minutes I had sunk the ship! After making this profound realization, I approached our relationship quite differently. I began to see her as a blessing sent to help me become more trustworthy. For years I had been working on developing this trait. I really did not like the way other people gossiped nor did I want to be a willing participant in idle slander. So I saw her as an answer to my request. Too bad I didn't get it sooner, because two weeks later, she quit and moved to Idaho. But as fate would have it, this job I am now doing as an energy worker requires someone who is completely trustworthy. No one is going to open up their most vulnerable wounds to someone they cannot inherently trust. How appropriate it was for me to have this blessing in my life for so many years before I began to apprentice with my teacher.

I include coworkers in a section of their own, because those of you who work with others will agree with me when I say they can be seriously challenging. Like spouses, coworkers can be people we spend a lot of time with and get to know very well, but unlike marriages, divorce doesn't end the relationship. Some people find it easier to divorce a spouse than to quit a job where there is an unbearable boss or coworker. If there are important issues at hand vital for your life's journey, an impossible coworker could literally be part of the majority of your physical life. We need to look at our coworkers in the same light as our partners and children and parents; as gifts sent to challenge and/or support us. The story about the woman who moved to Idaho still amazes me, because of all the people in that company, the only two I ever had any negative feelings for ended up being individuals sent to assist me far more than I ever could have comprehended at the time. I figured that once I left the company, I would never think twice about either one again, but in fact, I have been grateful to both in my thoughts more times than I remember our difficulties.

The second coworker/teacher showed up several years later. I had already begun working in energy healing and my life was shifting course. Even though I made good money and was putting my husband through a professional school, I knew my tenure at my day job was coming to an end. The comfort level was so high though—no conflict, great status, super coworkers, great pay—that the stimulus to actually take leave of this second family never really came. My comfortable chair phase, no doubt. Then, enter the Ice Queen. My company hired a woman to work in the accounting department. I tried to warm up to her and make her feel at home there, as I always would, but to no avail. After several weeks of thinking she was extremely shy, and getting no response from her whatsoever, I let it go. All I ever got from her was a piercingly cold stare. I didn't really avoid her, I just didn't include her. She took to dogging me. She wanted my approval and went about it in a unique way. She seemed to have eyes in the back of her head and whenever she got half a chance, she would complain about me to the owner of the company. I couldn't understand it. I talked to her personally, only to have her accuse me of wanting to see her fail and then she would leave crying. I became more baffled. All the efforts I made to try to connect were unsuccessful. This went on for several months. She dogged my trail, I tried to be invisible. Finally, I had a blow out with one of the owners who believed everything this new accounting manager fed him. I asked him if he'd ever gotten a complaint about me in the 10 years I had worked there, either from a coworker, a client, a vendor, or anyone else? He admitted that he never had. Why did he feel compelled to believe this new employee of only three months? The answer was not forthcoming from him. The answer had to come from me. Why? Because she was sent there for me to change directions in my life. And I did. That relationship created just enough discomfort to make the change seem suddenly more urgent. I understand from my friends who still work there that the Ice Queen found another job only a few months after I left, having done a superbly excellent job of sending me on. I have been thankful to her on many occasions as I enjoy my current life, feeling blessed to have had such a tenacious teacher.

One element that we have in a workplace is the issue of authority. Someone is your boss, you are someone else's boss, there are ranks of employees, management, VPs and so on. There is a hierarchy that in itself challenges. Once in my former life, in an attempt to create a responsibility or organizational chart, I used all my creative skills to try to represent who reported to whom without making it look like the pyramid that we all despise with the boss man on top, the lowly worker ants on the bottom. With a great deal of help from my husband, what I ended up with was a star chart. The owners were in the middle, with each phase of production, sales and accounting radiating out on its own beam until everyone was accounted for without anyone being on the 'bottom'. There is an ever-present balance of each person's ego involved in a structure as complex as the workplace. This, in fact, may be why most people can relate to the coworker-as-challenge issue. If there is a structure of accountability, there are probably egos to contend with. So I guess that means, unless you work for yourself in a bell jar, you are dealing with someone else's ego.

Here is where the subtle bodies come in again. Remember, there are those people who have overly developed their ego, some their mental body, some their emotional or physical body and some their soul. I am not suggesting that everyone who is a boss is egoic. Those who are fair and easygoing bosses probably don't come up when I talk about workplace teachers, but certainly can, depending upon the lesson required. The ones who challenge may not even be people in authority over you, but there is the conflict they represent, as with the Ice Queen. If we look out of the eyes of our egos and answer the question, *"What do I dislike most about that person?"* we can undoubtedly come up with some really un-kind responses, like I did with the woman who moved to Idaho. But when we look through the lens of the soul, that highest part of oneself, truly searching and wanting to grow, we may find that what we most dislike about that person is some aspect of *our own selves* that we are outgrowing.

Let's look at another example. I presently work with a client who got a new job in the marketing department of a large corpo-ration. She was very eager to prove herself and worked extra hard on the first few projects that she was given. She came up with some very creative ideas and presented them to her boss. Her boss loved them and they went forward developing them. Then when they were presented to the owner and upper management, this woman's boss took credit for my client's ideas as if they were from her own hard work. At first, she discounted the situation, thinking she was lucky just to have the job, so better not rock the boat. Then as time went on and this pattern became a reoccurring theme in her work life, she started wondering what she could do about it. More important than doing something about it, she could search for what she needs to learn. And it seems that when our egos are involved, it is painful learning. I don't know the final outcome, but the awarenesses I offered were that there is a desire unconsciously to be led away from the stranglehold of the ego, as well as a call to be able to honor oneself. She had to find a suitable solution to be able to cultivate and honor her creativity as well as not place too much importance on receiving public credit. In other words, she needed to assess whether she had placed her ego in control and find a place of balance in her life. Her issues were certainly being challenged, since these were essentially the main issues with which we had worked together.

One of my earliest clients used to change jobs fairly often and, over the course of the time we worked together, found himself in a repeating work situation. In each job he reported to an extremely dominant female. It made his life uncomfortable as he felt this female authority figure would undermine his efforts and force him to finally either relocate within the company or find employment elsewhere. But invariably, he would find himself reporting to another dominating female at the new position. The same energetic pattern replayed itself in every job. Quitting isn't always the answer because if it is time to look at certain issues illuminated by a particular personality trait, you may land right back in a similar environment. Perhaps this client's issues stemmed from childhood and his subjugation to his own dominant mother. Obviously he was ready on some level to move to a place of owning his own authority and the archetypally dominant female showed up for him acting as a spring board.

This brings me to my next point which is equality. In any workplace, there are those who invariably think they are above someone else, not just in position, but in skills or worth to the company or in net worth. As a recent ad in a magazine touts, "Don't confuse net worth with self-worth." As I mentioned earlier, when we are living in our highest selves, we remember that all souls are equal. You may not feel you are being treated as such, but on some level, that is the choice you have made. I have worked in companies where one department receives more benefits in the way of salary, accolades, extras, time off and so on than employees in another part of the company. It may be unspoken, or it may be written, the question you must ask yourself is why am I on this side of the company? Is this position upholding firm unconscious beliefs I have about my own self-worth? When you cease carrying the vibration that you are inferior or less than someone else, no one can make you feel inferior, it just won't take. Any coworker treating you as an inferior will be there until you heed that message. And at the same time, there will come a moment in your life when you stop looking at those who *you* feel are above you, or more valuable than you and see them through the lens of your soul, as equals.

Do you see the repeated message of responsibility? I believe you have made choices that you are now living out. The people who show up in your life are there for a reason. When you recognize what that is, not only does life become easier and fuller, you appreciate even the most seemingly insignificant relationships.

A woman I know tells a story of visiting an ailing neighbor. She truly liked the lonely old man even though he was a bit senile. On her last visit to the 89-year-old on his birthday, she confided that she had been thinking about what we had talked about, that there is something to learn from every relationship. She thought she was only there to keep him from being so lonesome and hopefully to share some joy together. She listened to him talk, and then she listened some more. My friend began to wonder where was the lesson to learn from this old man who still talks about the war and never stops telling his story? He never asks about me or inquires about my life. She suddenly realized that she also had a passion for telling stories, probably why she endured his so well, and she felt hers were very interesting, as I'm sure he did his. She then became overwhelmed with the gift of seeing herself as an 89-year-old woman, still telling her stories, never taking the time to ask about others or let them share their own stories. She silently thanked him for his birthday gift.

Relationships are the vehicles for drawing out our most creative selves because there is usually something valuable that the other person has that we want, whether it is a friendship or a job or acccptance, and we have something they want. So we are willing to go to the effort it requires for the return. We have to get past their ego front and they have to get past ours. These challenging relationships force us into our creative places, attempting verbal communication, which is limited, trying to connect egoically, which is hard, and ultimately giving up or giving it over to our highest self, which works in ways we could hardly imagine.

Let's look at bosses and authority figures. If your temperature is rising just thinking about them, you need to remember this all important question, "*How do they make me feel?*" After you have had an interaction with your most challenging boss and have returned to your work space, try to process the emotions you are feeling. What are they? Which ones can be attributed to not sleeping well or having undue financial stress, and which ones are the repeat performances of every interaction with this person? Identify *those* emotions, mark them for later, then take note of where they have set up residency in your energy system. If this boss is your 'headache' or your 'ulcer', you may want to pay a visit later.

For example, if someone is always hounding you about not being punctual, or finishing a project on time, or following up with your clients, and this bothers you, you may need to look at a lack of integrity stuck somewhere in your system. If you have no interest in changing your current level of personal responsibility or integrity, then continue on your present course. Just know this, if it bugs you, if you feel emotional (resentful or hurt) it is up for review, which means other teachers will come along if you choose to ignore the present one.

If you are being berated by a superior for doing an excellent job which then makes them look bad, you need to determine if you are truly honoring yourself as you should be. This may simply be an opportunity to stand up for your own personal integrity. There are millions of scenarios played by over six billion individuals on this planet, each with their own set of issues and their own personal soulful journey. Looking at your *own* unique baggage is the only way to heal, you can't heal anyone else anyway. Trust me, I have tried.

SIBLINGS AND RELATIVES

There's a whole new set of ways we can learn from relationships with sisters and brothers and more distant relatives like aunts and uncles. Being related, they seem to show up at family functions, or sometimes feel compelled to come and visit. You may not see them often, but there they are, toting their own personal button-pushing equipment. Or you may see them quite often and still have not found a way to have a smooth relationship. There seems to be accumulated baggage adding to the weight of these long-term relationships. I personally like to travel and have moved a lot. Each time I move to a different state, to a different community, I can renew myself. Moving affords a person the opportunity to bring with them what they love about themselves and leave behind the older, tired parts that no longer have a role in their life. It is refreshing and allows one's highest attributes to keep surfacing. Family, however, can hold memories that make it more difficult to embody this newly created person. This is part of our family's personal armament, and believe me, we are holding similar baggage about them. Remember the wedding I told you about where my whole family attended? What I specifically did to try to energetically bring some healing and love into the experience was to work on egoic images. Egoic images are just that, images or ways of seeing others that our ego holds about them. We imagine them to be true because of an experience or repeated experiences that made us believe a certain way. There really isn't an expiration date on egoic images, even though I wish there were.

I found that I had some images of the sister getting married dating back to 1981! That was 20-some years before. I believed quite firmly (egoically) that she was stupid and embarrassing. I had to look into 1981 and see what was going on back then. At that time she was getting married to a guy I considered a negative asset, and I also thought she was too young to get married in the first place. So I unconsciously programmed my egoic body to believe that she would always to be thought of as stupid. Egoic images are not programmed consciously, which makes their removal a bit more sticky. Now, many years later, she had divorced her husband, wised up, according to my judgmental mind, finished college, held positions in her work life of major responsibility, but inside my energetic system that programming still ran the 'stupid' factor. So I talked to myself and convinced myself to step back into 1981, or, rather, bring the energy of 1981 to the present day, and undo or de-program that egoic image. It is amazing how it works. I found that I really have had a lot more respect for her since doing that. I also found that most of my other family members were passing their own judgment on her from 1981. She obviously was challenging our consensus reality! I spoke to their higher selves about letting go of those images. In a later chapter I'll suggest how to talk to someone's higher self.

Our family challenges us most by holding antiquated images of us. You may have grown immensely since you were 13, but Aunt Georgia is still retelling the story of you running away from home and smoking pot or something equally as antique. Here's the challenge. If it elicits an emotional response, there is still something unhealed there. If you can say, "Aunt Georgia, I really didn't just smoke pot, I threw beer cans off the Junction Bridge and got a tattoo of Rush Limbaugh on my butt!" and can watch her turn red and not think another thing about your 13-year-old experience, there is no healing that needs to happen there. If however, you lay into her and start screaming for her to shut up about when you were 13, and threaten that if she ever retells that story again you will personally assist with her timely euthanasia, then I am going to make a stab in the dark that there is something unresolved about your experience. Maybe you haven't forgiven yourself for hurting your mother, maybe you can't forgive yourself for doing something you now consider irresponsible, or maybe you can't forgive yourself for coming back! This is the beauty of family. They knew you since you were knee high to a grasshopper, remember?

The other aspect of family, especially siblings, is that they have also been a witness to your life. They have lived through many of the same experiences and watched you fumble and watched you succeed, and many times, they still love you anyway. I think that about my sister who is closest to my age. We were not terribly kind to each other while growing up. I was stubborn and finicky. She was irresponsible and careless. We tried life out on each other, we were mean, we were caring, we were everything to each other at one time or another over the years *and* we still love each other dearly. You can believe that maybe you're not going to rot in hell for what you did when you were 19 if your sister knows about it and has forgiven you and still loves you. Then you can say, just maybe who I am is forgivable and maybe even worth the effort. In the meantime, we still keep trying our new ideas about life on each other. Sometimes when we can't see it ourselves, they can remind us just how much we have changed and grown for the better.

It is more difficult to disentangle your own issues from those of your closest siblings. Having shared intense emotions together on numerous occasions, discerning what belongs to you and what is theirs may not be crystal clear. Often we buy into our sibling's modes of operation. Manipulating through guilt or taking advantage of vulnerabilities are just two ways to get what we want and at the same time provide an opportunity for growth for the other person involved. Intelligent dark energies don't even need to be present in a family situation, because we have all become experts at identifying and perfectly recalling our sibling's deepest fears or weaknesses.

Expectations are all a part of that baggage of family stuff. This can be quite challenging. For example, many people I know dread Thanksgiving because there is an expectation from their family to attend a group dinner or weekend when they don't feel up to it or really don't enjoy that kind of get-together anyway. In fact, my husband who works in healing sees a great increase in calls during the holidays since family stress equals back and neck pain. As soon as the holidays are over, everyone miraculously feels so much better. I moved away from my immediate family when I was 20 and never really had to make decisions about holidays because I lived across the continent, but my husband's family was another matter. I really enjoyed them and their get-togethers. But they weren't *my* family, so consequently, they didn't have access to my buttons like my own family did. My husband dreaded the holiday get-togethers like the rest of America. After we were married a few years, I asked him why we did these family functions if they were so painful to him. He replied that it was expected of him. Expected by whom? Would someone in his family really want him to attend if they knew how he hated the organized, obligated rituals? No. So we made a decision about expectations: we would only try to meet our own individual ones, and no one else's. Now we love Thanksgiving. We are one of the few couples we know that have the most delightful, nonconflictual Thanksgiving with much smaller quantities of food.

Skipping holidays with the family can be empowering, but it doesn't mean you can avoid the issues that your family lights up for you. Siblings are different from parents because they don't really hold authority over you, or not as much as a parent anyway. There may be issues of jealousy or rivalry, of being made to feel less than another family member in a comparative way. All for the purpose, I think, to get you to own your personal, unique gifts. My brother and I were talking on the phone the other day when he said, "You know, everything used to be great between us until *Jan* was born!" I said "What? I was *two* when Jan was born." He said, "Yeah, well, we were best friends, we did everything together, and you really liked me, then your little *sister* was born and all that was ruined!" I know he was half joking, but part of him remembered a time when it was just the two of us with no competition from anyone else.

Issues of comparing and contrasting are sibling issues. Those issues are ones the ego perpetuates too, so to get beyond them, you have to have a chat with your own private Kirk or ego. Then you can delve into the drawing room of the active thing that needs attention. If you find yourself feeling less than your highest self when you are around a particular sibling or relative, try the same question we use for bosses and coworkers. How do they make me feel? You may be surprised that what you think is not actually what is registering in your energy system. In my energy sessions, I monitor clients' words and they often don't match the energy I am picking up. A common example is a client who has issues with a particular family member. When asked specifically about that relationship, they offer me the pre-prepared answer that they don't even think of that person anymore. They suggest that they long ago stopped having issues with that person, they simply "wrote them off." Finale, done, kaput, just like that, or so they think. Their energy reads something very different. Only you can determine if it is worth the price it may require to sort out the meaning of the relationship and grow from it.

Obligation, like expectation, can be crippling in the family relationship game. If you feel obligated to support a family member in a way that conflicts with your ethics or financial situation or any number of things, it can bring such resentment into the relationship that it harms both of you by engaging in it. For example, if you are asked to lie about the living arrangements of another family member to mom and dad, but you don't feel comfortable or honest doing that, it challenges your own personal ethics. You have a unique situation. There is the obligation and responsibility that you feel towards family, ingrained since birth, and then there is the sense of personal responsibility you have nurtured since you were old enough to think for yourself. This situation challenges your *true* ethics, not just what you espouse. If your sister asks to borrow money you know she has no way of paying back and you are not all right with that, to do it challenges you. It forces you to ask yourself, would I rather live with my own internal anger at putting myself in a difficult financial situation than risk the anger of a sibling who believes I *ought* to do this for her? Either way you feel bad, unless you resolve what it is that bugs you most about this request. Is it really the finances? Maybe. If it were a medical emergency, you would gladly throw in what you could and a little more. What is it? It is against your ethics to disempower another person by making them dependent on someone else for their support. There it is. That's really what is bugging you. You have been working on this for years, trying to learn that others are capable human beings, and can function perfectly well without your help. You suddenly feel a hook drawing you back from your growth curve. It doesn't feel good. Depending on what you decide, you either land yourself back on wobbly ground with that issue or solidly push over the edge to terra firma.

Forgiveness is a key element arising with extended family members. People you don't see very often can go on with their lives, with or without you, so you never really have to address anything about them. They are not intimate enough to make life personally painful to you. You just hear something trashy about them third hand from Aunt Carol. Then when they show up, at a family function or event, memories of your last conversation with Aunt Carol resurface too. It may have been 12 years since this evil event transpired, but you are still holding the memory of it, and though it may not even be true, it colors your view of this person. Everyone has a relative who has transgressed, done something others consider heinous, jeez, it might even be you or me. Those closest to that person have had to forgive and forget and go on, but those of us who aren't so close can continue to hold this morbid memory that, like an egoic image, serves only to hold the growth of this person solidly in the past.

When these relatives physically resurface in our lives, it may well be for the purpose of exercising forgiveness. At my last family function, one cousin asked me how I could be so nice to so and so after what he had done to his wife 15 years ago. Wow, I had to try to remember. Oh yeah, I had struggled with those same issues of self-honor myself and knew how he was challenging her, whereas my cousin had different issues and was not yet willing to forget his misdeeds. If we wish to be forgiven and our past forgotten, we must be prepared to do the same for others. When I was thinking about the images I held about my sister from 1981 I knew that I personally didn't want someone judging *me* from 1981. The more emotionally indignant you feel yourself becoming in the presence of this wayward family member, the more important it is to look and see what it is about their deed that you abhor. Do you unconsciously treat others this same way? Do you find others treating you this way and you lack the courage to stand up for yourself? Do you dislike being judged by others who don't know the whole story about you, yet find yourself judging this very fellow, convicted on hearsay alone?

I don't propose to cover the complexities of forgiveness, but I do offer it as a real challenge that families pose. I worked with an older man about issues he had with his family from some years back. At the end of our session, I told him that we could not go on until he cut some negative cords to his father, long deceased, by forgiving him. He said he was not willing to do that, that what his father had done to all of his siblings and himself he could *never* forgive. I talked about forgiveness for about 15 minutes, but he wasn't budging. Finally, I said, "Do you want to be connected to your father forever? Into the next realm and the next?" He said, "No, absolutely not!" I said, "Well, you will be since you have a huge black cord connecting you to him. It doesn't mean that you condone what he did, you simply exercise your divine right to forgive and in doing so, that cord falls away." He said, "Let's do it."

Allow your body to be an *issue barometer*. When you feel stressed, irritated or emotional, look around you. What is either happening or about to happen that could be creating these unique opportunities? Perhaps you just need to remove some of your daily obligations to find a more manageable level. Are there certain people that bring with them the same uncomfortable, bodily reaction on your part? Remember to look at how *you* feel, not what others are or aren't doing to you.

7 Turning Back the Clock: Social Influences

Just as you are dealing with people and their package plans, you are also influencing others and helping to create who they are. Whether you are a parent or have friends or are a boss or a lover, you are influencing others. What I want to investigate are the ways, conscious and not, that we become who we are and the reasons behind those choices. First, so that we can become aware of the conditioning or beliefs we no longer want to carry, and second, so that we can stop the cycle, if possible, of continuing to sponsor patterns or beliefs that are just that, beliefs and not truths.

A woman I know has one of the most unusual syndromes I have come across. I called it the Iceberg Effect. She is mostly hidden from view, not physically, but energetically. Let's turn back the clock. While her mother was pregnant with her, a strange battle over the man who was her biological father ensued, and to make the story short, this woman's mother was left husbandless.

Not only that, but the woman who stole the heart, or at least the body, of the biological father wanted absolutely nothing to do with his former lover.

The legal wife forbade him from ever contacting his ex-lover and was unaware that there was a child from this former union (great basis for a new relationship, huh?) The father, however, wanted to keep in contact with his child if at all possible, but the baby was kept a secret. He did the best he could, sending money and support to his invisible offspring, but never allowing his daughter to meet or see his other legitimate family. She came to know and visit him, and over the years formed a belief that this was a fairly normal way of having a relationship with one's father. Here we are 50 years later and she doesn't understand why she is invisible. When she is present at a teacher's meeting and forms or papers are passed out, inevitably, she is always skipped. When she is in line waiting her turn, she is always overlooked, the person behind her taken first. She has come to expect it and even her teeth have responded to this strange belief. She has extremely large roots and very small teeth, like an iceberg, creating a multitude of difficulties for the dentist. Her teeth have been rotting from the roots up. There's a symbolic message right here, isn't there? The roots of your own personal history are beginning to sabotage you. The point is, as a very young child, she was kept a secret by her own father, the one we all expect to honor and love us and who helped create us. Her energy system responded to this belief the best it could, believing as she did that it was in her best interest to be invisible. Fifty years later, she really is energetically invisible and can't understand why.

This story illustrates how, in one life, we can see results of interpretations of previous experiences. I prefer to go back further than that, but it gets more entwined. Who remembers before this life and who really can verify that we have ever existed before? Another belief we must tolerate! I believe that there is a reason that she came into the life of a man who would have a lover, who would have another lover who would become his wife, and so on, for the purpose of working out something in her own karmic baggage. For the purposes of this work, I will try to stick to present day issues. Suffice it to say, however, that very possibly choices we make before we are in our human, egoic self could lend significantly to the things that happen to us in this present life.

What about those who were adopted? Almost all the individuals I work with who have been adopted carry the vibration of worthlessness or some variation of that theme. Maybe unlovable or not valuable, but it persists throughout adulthood plaguing their intimate relationships, jobs, and talents. Does this mean we should outlaw adoption? Not at all. Does this mean adopted parents aren't really kind and loving? Absolutely not. In many cases I have known the parents and they couldn't love their adopted children more if they were of their own flesh and blood. It doesn't matter. It is part of the adopted child's preprogrammed baggage. So don't take it personally when you are trying to love or support an adopted adult and they continue to sabotage their own successes. It is part of what they need to work out, something valuable in this existence while others in their life have their own unique learning experiences.

One woman I worked with a few years ago had serious issues of self-esteem because she was a child born to a couple who financially could not afford having her and she energetically picked up their conversations in utero. She came in feeling she was a burden and unwanted. Was this created simply from picking up energetically on one conversation? I don't suspect so. I find that the amount of energy or emotion around an issue or concern dictates the quality of that belief. A person can have a repeat performance of the same energy situation and not attach a personal belief to it until what I call the *straw that broke the camel's back*. Then for whatever reason, something clicks in, as a method of interpreting existence perhaps, and it becomes a personal belief. It is then that we must live under its strict jurisdiction for it operates as a truth for us.

Another client felt the pang of disappointment when her parents found out she was a girl and carried issues of being a second-class citizen, less than men, her whole life. I am not insinuating we should walk on eggshells, what I am suggesting is that the way we have viewed the physical world, with our five senses, may be only part of the problem. To overlook the strongest link to our system, energy, unseen and perhaps sensorily undetectable, is a grave mistake. Also, knowing that others are working out their karma, or reaping the seeds they have sown, does not mean we should have any less compassion for them. Our understanding and concern and love for them are often the tide that turns the ship from its self-destructive course.

Let's look at some other sources of early belief management. Keep in mind, this is for you to find the keys to your own past as well as to contemplate how you may be part of the problem or part of the solution.

EDUCATION

If you talk to adults about their childhood the thing that invariably makes them cringe is that time of their life when they were ostracized or embarrassed by someone they looked up to or trusted. In schools we have a whole collection of young, evolving people all situated in the same container. Let's take a look at the way school is set up. It's about competition and separation. We are each asked to perform the best we can, but we are constantly compared to every other individual there and are ranked according to our performance, regardless if it is the best we can do. So we are set at odds with our fellow students through a list of "don'ts." Don't help them get the answers, it is only through their own hard efforts that they succeed. Don't share a newfound resource, or they may uncover information that may make your work look less exceptional. Don't work together, or one person will invariably take advantage of the other. Don't chew gum while taking a test, because your body will automatically go out of the flight or fight mode and you may be able to actually send much needed blood to the brain. There are many examples, not because any one person is trying to make life harder or intends to make us feel like we need to compete, but simply because of the nature of how education got set up a long time ago. I think there is this feeling that we are being prepared for life, but maybe education is instead setting up the rules for life. What about cooperation and teamwork? What about nurturing the concept that we all belong to the same unity of humans on the planet? What about a completely new way of enlightening our young and opening their minds without limitations, fitting into boxes or conforming? What about a way to nurture the unique creativity that is present in all of us as young people, but soon gets squelched when trying to bloom in an unsafe, critical environment. Maybe the world that we are being prepared for would be different.

I teach a workshop in opening the creative channels by using watercolor painting as a mode of creative expression. One of the first things we do is identify those individuals or incidents in our earliest memories that made us feel bad when we expressed ourselves creatively, whether that was making a mud sculpture or a finger painting or a mural on mom's wall. Again and again with every group, as soon as they started in public school they began the process of closing down. For as long as many could remember, they believed that they were either not creative or should not express their own creative self for fear of negative repercussions.

Anyway, given the nature of present day school and the educational system, this is the environment in which we find ourselves. Anticipating the potential difficulties of any given day, unable and not confident enough to feel prepared for *any* eventuality, we are sent off to school with a sense of dread. Even the term 'sent to school' implies a serious lack of choice in that department by the sendee. As young and fragile individuals, we are asked to conform to some norm that does not seem to express the true self of anyone I know.

Michael Moore, in his recent documentary film entitled *Bowling for Columbine* about violence in America, interviews a few high school students on their opinions about being in high school. They all had choice words, but the bottom line was, "it sucked." They admitted that they got picked on, made fun of and humiliated. And in turn did the same thing to other students. What creates this expression of belittling others to make our own selves look better?

My opinion is the way education is structured ingrains competition, difference and judgment from day one. Have you ever gone to a park and watched toddlers play? They never distinguish between races or sexes. The only criterion is that their playmates are also children. But as soon as they start to school, they realize there are differences and usually start segregating themselves according to class, creed, sex and/or race. We are separated according to our age, sex, religion and geographical area. This has to influence the way we think and what we feel we ought to do to conform. I am not here to write a thesis on the new education of America. I simply am shining some light on what makes us who we are.

I wonder about the future self-esteem of my 7-year-old grandson who, in a classroom of 48 students, is Magic Number 20. Not Travis Scott Luke, inventor, creator, reader, hero sledder, quilter, trampoline jumper extraordinaire, but Magic Number 20. On all his papers, this is what he writes. This is how he is addressed. I know personally, as I read the list of how *I* see him, it makes me feel I am in the presence of a super hero, whereas Magic Number 20 leaves me a bit cold and feeling like I am stuck in the worst that science-fiction has to offer. We are products of this institution whether we liked it or not. We learned how to manage through it, kept our heads down and our lights under a bushel so as not to attract too much attention for fear of ridicule or embarrassment. The possibility exists to be able to undo some of the negative effects of early conditioning, if we are conscious of it and if we attempt to recreate a new reality. If you have children, being aware of the squelching of their souls that may be happening during school hours, and by reinforcing their unique traits, you will be offering some appreciation for them as unique, special people. Then maybe they won't need to hide their own beautiful attributes for the sake of conformity.

We are taken as a group, a grade, taught what that grade should know, according to what some educators somewhere think, without any concern for what may be natural propensities or desires that don't necessarily adhere to a particular age group. In fact, until high school, there is very little, if any, choice associated with learning. Everyone knows that you learn faster and easier if it is something you like and you have an interest in it. If I just use my own nieces and nephews as examples, not to mention the many students I have worked with, I am assured of the diversity of us all. One nephew is interested in history, wars and battles. Another nephew from the same family is obsessed with bugs, creatures that jump and any slimy, crawly thing. Still another nephew excels at art. My niece is a brilliant, creative thinker and visionary. Does education provide the experiences for them to follow these desires, or must we as their mate/sibling/friend/relative lend a hand where formal education leaves off and help create an opportunity of support and fulfillment?

Each of us in our search for self-identity and acceptance is unconsciously looking for material with which we can make the fibers of ourselves. Who are we? What makes us special? What makes us unique? Unfortunately, we are looking to the very ones who are still looking for who *they* are, our peers. All the other young people surrounded by the walls we call school are growing and learning and wanting to find out who they are too. As we traveled around the United States, my husband made an interesting observation coming into any given town. He often said, "Well, that building is either the county jail, or the high school." At first we joked about it, but after a few more towns and a lot more states realized there was more truth in it than humor. I did notice that the jails, even though they had bars on the windows, did seem to have more windows. I remember as a young teen trying to find out if the rumor was true that it was raining and we wouldn't have outside PE. It would take several hours and several classes before I'd have a class in a windowed room and could actually look out and see the weather. So in looking for where we accumulate the bits and pieces of who we believe we are, don't forget to look back to those formative years of education.

CREATING A SAFE HAVEN

The thing I want to impress most about being an individual is the process of beginning to express ourselves. It is not only an integral part of how we were able to grow or were stifled, it is also a huge part of present relationships. Providing a safe, noncritical environment when someone we care about is expressing themselves is elementary in just communicating, not to mention nurturing someone's creativity. We all develop habits from early childhood that are responses to something. If we were praised, we repeated that act. If we were disciplined, we omitted that, even if it happened to be our most creative nature. It usually *is* our most creative nature. I am singling out education because it is our first contact with organized discipline and structured molding, but it could happen anywhere.

Imagine that you are a young soul, developing, opening, exploring, and reaching out to touch those things that make you feel the best. Guided by your natural intuition, listening to your tummy, you eat when you're hungry and sleep when you're tired; so human, so natural, so balanced. Then we get sent off to be with a whole group of people like us, budding artists, scientists, inventors, poets, but the hostility that most of us are greeted with begins to close those fragile creative doors of expression. Creativity is the expression of the soul, and the soul is the core of who we are. And do we want the core of who we are ridiculed or stomped on or ignored? A friend told a story about her five-year-old grandson that illustrates a potential challenge. One fine Sunday morning, this self-thinking five-year-old announced to his father that he wasn't going to go to church. He said, "I don't want to go to church. It ruins my whole day, no, it ruins my *whole life!*" His father succinctly redirected his son's thought process to one that accommodated his *own* way of thinking and so continued to offer up the challenges we create for ourselves in the Earth School. What message does that send to our young thinker? The feelings you feel are *wrong*? They are not permitted? Sitting in a boring, sedate audience listening to things you cannot understand and do not resonate with is *right*? *Show* me that god is love, don't *tell* me about it! Let me know it for myself instead of you telling me how I should feel, but don't. Who is being challenged? Ultimately, it will be both father and son if that is the role they are to play in each others' life.

So many times I hear teachers inputting their opinions as if there were no other way, as if it were fact instead of emotionally-based opinions. Young minds look up to these authority figures their parents have told them to mind, and they begin the process of closing down their own intuitive way for the more accepted way of their teacher.

I spent the first several weeks of my university art class convincing the students that we weren't going to trash each others' work during critique time. They didn't believe me for a long time, but finally after several weeks with no deviation from this rule, the students in my watercolor class were able to open up because they weren't being graded on how well they could render, or make a tree look like a tree, or how close to the teacher's own style they came. They were realizing that the object was expressing with watercolor what they wanted to say, or feel or see. It was an amazing project for me with equally amazing results. These students had a set of criteria for critiquing their own and their fellow students' artwork. What is the artist trying to express? How are they doing it; through color, medium, style, contrast? What are the emotions being emitted? And what is the favorite part of the painting? It was too simple, they were being graded on expressing themselves. I had monitored the feedback the first few weeks to make sure that someone didn't yell out, "That's stupid and ugly." No one did and everyone responded to this kind of safe environment in a relatively short time, considering how many years of opposite experiences many had.

One day, I was on the far side of the classroom when I suddenly felt the room go cold. Everyone stiffened and the safeness felt compromised. I looked up and around the room trying to comprehend what had just caused this. I saw just then a fellow teacher who had waltzed into the room and was standing over the shoulder of one student while he was painting. Before I could get over to him, he had spewed, "What is *that* supposed to be?" I felt the student recoil and make a witty remark, but the teacher was not backing off. This teacher, I had heard from the other students, was brutally critical in all his art classes. I gently ushered him to the door to see what he wanted.

Another student always left his paint supplies on the table after class was over, but I never understood why. I knew he was not absentminded, but could not figure why he would leave all his tools to have to come back later. One afternoon I was staying late to collect something for the class when this particular student came back in. I asked him why he did this so often. A very sensitive and gentle person, he answered that this class was such a safe haven for him that he hated thinking it was over. So he would leave things to come back for later in the day just to be able to step back into this creative safe haven again.

I know that life isn't like that. Even though I wish it would be. But if we would provide a safe haven at home, for our children, our spouses, our parents, how much more could our souls express themselves? How beautiful would that be? Have you ever seen someone express their soul and have it be negative? I personally never have. Egos will do that, but souls are divine. What if we made a conscious decision to all honor the soul and allow the expression of ourselves and others free reign? If we are to be everything we can be, and inspire our significant other or our offspring, how could we do that while being critical? Maybe that is the way you were raised, or your spouse was raised, but it does *not* provide fertile soil for the growth of the soul. If you look back into your own childhood, you will undoubtedly remember fondly those who supported you when everyone else thought your idea was crazy, or inspired you with their own creativity, against all societal norms.

To create a safe haven, this is what you do. You identify when someone is expressing themselves, whether verbally or visually or productively. You sense what they are communicating. You hear what they are not saying, you feel what they are emoting, or whatever you are capable of doing, to whatever degree you can. But you *don't* laugh or scoff or ridicule or turn away. You provide a safe haven for the soul. That doesn't mean you have to like what they express, or even appreciate it. That is not the point, if it is the expression of self, it deserves honor. It may just be the beginning of finding the front end of this soul stuff and may be crude or crass, but it is a seed in the stage of germinating. Don't crush it or dry it out before it has even made one root. I once read a biography of Andrew Wyeth (the 20th century watercolorist from the Northeast) and even though he has enjoyed great fame in this life with his work, he still does not like anyone to make any comments at all about his paintings before he is done. Once just the absence of any comment from his wife, who looked over his shoulder, made him feel she did not like it and he never finished the painting. Now imagine how it might be with less famous personages. Until I started these nontraditional methods with my watercolor class, I did not realize how often we generally criticize each other as a natural part of our relationships. My husband has never considered himself an artist in drawing, but once was outlining a picture in the steam of the glass shower door. When I heartily laughed, he said, "Hey, what about providing a safe environment here?" I was ashamed. Even laughing in inappropriate moments can be brutal. I have known people who remember that laugh for years.

What does it mean to be critical, and when is it okay to take a difference of opinion? When you are exchanging opinions, then by all means, share yours. But when someone is expressing the contents of their soul, honoring, instead of criticizing, creates the most inspiring material for deep relationships. Sometimes we are so conditioned to a certain response or belief in the way the world *is* that we ignore the possibility that there may not be a right or wrong. There most likely will be something that challenges you though. This is the nature of relationships, remember? The very places in which you unconsciously are asking for expansion and breadth are the places you will be challenged the most. You need to be available for this lesson and by being available, it means not coming at every transaction with a win/lose attitude. Try to invite a share/share energy situation. This is how you do it. You honor yourself and you honor the other. You try to look at every interaction as an opportunity to really *hear* the other person, and to imagine that their way *may* have particular merits you hadn't thought about. In fact, if you are having the discussion, there is probably a reason. (I happen to believe that there are no coincidences). No interrupting or scoffing is permitted. Jumping to conclusions is off limits. Opening your mind to the extent to which it is capable is required. Creating a safe haven for your loved ones, your coworkers, or your students or wherever you work/play/exist, is a really wonderful way to begin to let the lessons flow and the relationships flower.

AUTHORITY FIGURES

Let's look at some other individuals imprinting our beautiful souls. I have an image of young people, trying to figure out who and what they are, carrying around an empty mirror. They look for others to reflect something in it, perhaps some part of who they want to be or feel they could be. I see this *creation mirror* as aiding in the development of their self-esteem, or the lack thereof. Teachers, counselors, ministers and coaches all play their part in assisting young people grow and mature in a healthy way depending upon what they show this empty mirror. In fact, they carry more authority, because they *are* authority figures, and not only to youth. They are generally regarded by our society as role models and guides. Automatically, our already vulnerable and impressionable young people give these figures more authority than they would to just anyone. It is not an uncommon scene to witness a student poking around for authenticity in role models and pulling back a stump. When you find a teacher or counselor with unresolved issues of power or acceptance for example, a developing young mind may push the wrong button and get, not a refection of the potential that student can grow up to be, but a glimpse of an unresolved issue that still needs healing from the teacher's own past. Ouch! The student then misreads this intense, emotional outburst as belonging to them (role models can't be wrong, can they?) not understanding that the teacher or counselor is human too.

I had an experience with my own high school counselor, whom I deeply adored. Back then, anything she said was the immortal word to me. She was from a big east-coast city, had a very sophisticated accent (so I thought at the time), and dressed in a very cosmopolitan manner, which was all I needed to form my opinion of her. I began to share more and more with her throughout each interaction and finally, one day, she said something that crushed me. I shared a dream I had that I *was* going to do, my whole 17-year-old self was sure of it. She laughed and scoffed at me, saying those were the dreams of a young person, but reality would find me doing something very different. She said it was hard to hold onto dreams like that in the real world. Well, that was *her* reality, not mine. I began to distance myself from her. I no longer felt safe and empowered when I was around her and began to question my own motives and beliefs. Could I really be who I wanted to be? Was life so brutal that it was going to crush my dreams? The one person I trusted to guide me (she was a *guidance* counselor) turned out to be the one jading my impression of the world, making me doubt my innocent ability to cope in a world without shields or weapons.

Well, strange as it may seem, every time I heard that scoff it deepened my resolve to never lose sight of that dream. And truthfully, she was probably right, given regular, adult life, I probably would have lost focus on that dream and replaced it with another. But to this day, I still remember the promise to myself to fulfill that dream. Perhaps, as I think of it, this book is part of living out that dream in a more comprehensive way. My dream was that I would *never* lose sight of the promptings of my own heart and that I would always make a light in this world that was compelled from my own inner stirrings. Regardless of what society said about me or what seemed right or wrong in someone else's mind, I would stay firm to the truth of my own self. Whew. Now that I think about it, it *is* a perfect world. Her scoffing at me pushed those words deep into the cells of my being, never to be forgotten, if for no other reason than to prove her wrong!

I wonder where I would be if she had *empowered* me. If she, with the unknown authority I had given her, had said, "Yes, that is possible and this much more. You can do it. I believe you can. It is a worthy goal to have and I will support you in it." It might not have taken me 25 years to truly embody it. Who knows? Or maybe I would have forgotten it, without the challenge she posed.

Teachers are fragile humans who have chosen to assist and nurture our youth into adulthood. They are constantly, year after year, bombarded with the call to see who they are and what they are made of by their young budding student population, so that after a while, some of them, no doubt, close the door to letting others look in. You can believe that one or two times they were embarrassed or humiliated while sharing their inner selves with the precious, yet brutal young products of the institution. So, either they appear stoic and unfeeling (as a means of protecting their delicate inner selves) or they show an artificial self to this group of questioners. Either way, we don't get to see the quality human being they are, that made them chose this occupation, which compels them to help and assist and teach young minds. What we see is a wall, understandably so.

All of us have had first-year, young teachers (I was one myself) who are so enthusiastic and fun and full of the stories and witty remarks that make class fun. It doesn't take too many years to either push them out of teaching (as in my case) or to make them realize they don't want to be hurt and humiliated, and find a less fun, but efficient protection. I remember from my school days two such teachers. One was a young French teacher. She was pretty, fun and enthusiastic. She shared her stories of adventure from France, studying French and her exciting relationships. Several times I can also recall an angry student making some rude remark afterwards to the effect of, "Who cares?" The reaction of our enthusiastic young teacher was to clam up and feel embarrassed after sharing a sincere personal story, and then being insulted with a rude comment. After several more repeated incidents, she probably spent more time on the assigned (safe) lesson plan and not on divergent stories and tales. She only lasted one year and I was very sad about that. We were left with an older teacher for the following three years of French who, I see now, had long since retreated within for protection. Those classes were not nearly as much fun. They were painful, actually.

In looking at the young man who issued the rude comment, however, I now have a greater understanding of what was going on inside his head. He most likely was someone who felt very unspecial. His only way to get the attention that he so craved was to interject significant mood changes into peaceful or vulnerable spots. He probably didn't feel adequate or intelligent enough to do it during an academic moment, feeling *he* would be the humiliated one, not the teacher. With so many subtleties going on, how are we to be aware and observant without taking them personally? We'll get to that later.

Let's first take a look at our other young teacher who didn't last long either. He was an English teacher and drama coach. He was very interesting looking, not exactly a knockout, but his personality was so exuberant that many of the young girls were attracted to him. It was his energy that people wanted to be around. As he unfolded his life in English class the young girls became more and more enamored with him and finally, he had a small cult following. Eventually, even though he was very professional and tried to deal with it the best he could, the administration spoke to him about drawing back his likeable personality to avoid any inappropriate scandal. Once again, we have the energetic youthful role model closing in, reflecting nothing in our impressionable mirrors.

I have worked with a number of adults who as teens were molested or abused by someone who assumed authority in their lives, perhaps a minister, a coach or a policeman. Sometimes it was a relative or another adult that they trusted. Most of the time, the reason I was working with them was to remove the negative effects of their imprinting some misunderstandings based on these situations where there was a terrible misuse of power; again the products of measuring, weighing and comparing. In this case, it is our personal worth or value. When we give someone authority over us, we set up an unequal relationship. They have their own power, we have given them some of ours, and then they end up with more power than a single individual should have. They are on a higher pedestal, we are on the lower one. It is either from class, race, sex, perceived intelligence or position. Let me ask you this: Is it necessary to give authority to someone to learn from them? To listen to someone? To honor someone? Couldn't we treat each other as equals, even if I am twelve and you are 66? I have never in my short life been in a relationship, no matter *how* short, how young or old, teacher or student, parent or child, male or female where there wasn't something to learn from the other. I have found that infants can teach us stress-free living. Kindergartners can teach us priorities. Young readers can teach us what we take for granted. Grandmas allocated to the nursing home can teach us patience and if we listen, things that are more important in life than we might think.

I imagine the only way we can do this is to see each other through the lens of the soul. That means bypassing the multifaceted and all encompassing personality of the ego, not buying into its façade, but instead seeing directly into the soul. That is the only place we find equality.

I did a project a few years ago where I tried to improve my vision by going a year without any corrective lenses. My vision had progressively deteriorated since I was 10 years old and I came to the point where I would not accept this as an inevitable fact of life and aging. During that year, I got pretty good at seeing what the face was not expressing, mainly because I couldn't *see* the face. One time, my husband and I went to visit a couple who were friends of ours. There was another friend of theirs visiting that we didn't know. They invited us in, and introduced us to this fellow. I could feel my husband keep a pretty large energetic distance between himself and this man. I attributed it to the fact that my husband is hard to get to know, and was just being reserved. I noticed that this new guy, even though I couldn't really get a bead on how old he was or much about what he looked like, spent the whole evening with a guitar in front of his body. This made me aware of a certain insecurity that made me sense his fragility. I moved right in on him, talking, asking questions, making us all feel more comfortable together. He really warmed up and started singing and playing and we had a great time. I connected right to his soul, same as mine, fragile and beautiful. Later that night, my husband asked me how I knew this guy was going to be so friendly, since his external self was transmitting the message "keep away" so strongly. I didn't catch that because I couldn't see the façade. A year later, when I could visually see again, I ran into this man in town, and was also surprised that I had opened up to him. His outward appearance certainly did not convey the openness that his soul had. He even startled me a bit re-meeting him, but he warmed right up after a smile and the remembrance of our shared friendship.

What I am saying is twofold. First, there are established authority figures in our society. Do you want them to be in your life? Are you losing power to any of them? Is that okay with you? Do you really believe someone's soul is better than yours? And second, if you can't change them (by the way, you can't), change the way you *see* them. Don't let the fierce, authoritative exterior sell you something you don't want to buy. Most people will not actually *take* your power, so don't give it up at the first sign of an aggressive-looking face. Connect with peoples' souls and you suddenly see people for the delicate, loving, soulful beings they are, no matter *what* their egos try to convince you.

NATIONAL FEAR

This is a topic that I am going to briefly touch on as a basis for helping us understand who we are. I believe fear colors more of our present world than we are conscious of. In the documentary I mentioned earlier about violence in America, *Bowling for Columbine*, after a comprehensive search for the underlying reason there is more gun violence in America than anywhere else on the planet, one of the proposals Michael Moore makes is that we live in a country abounding with fear. It is an underlying theme in America, from the news media, advertising, political platforms, the educational system to video games and movies. It is a constant bombardment if you live and breathe and read and observe in America. Advertising ads create fear of getting old, getting fat, having osteoporosis, sagging breasts, dry skin, dull hair, balding heads, less enviable vehicles than our neighbors and being left alone, in order to sell their products. The medical institution propagates the fear that we are one foot away from a heart attack, cancer, high blood pressure, cataracts, irritable bowel syndrome, fibromyalgia and that mysterious untreatable, incurable illness that could creep up if we don't take all our pills in a certain order, to sell their products. Our teachers feed us the fear that if we don't test well (as measured by them) in school we will invariably be a loser forever, doomed to a McJob if we're lucky. Our politicians use, as their political platform, fears of not being safe, needing more security, impending crisis and takeover of the American way if we don't eradicate anyone and everything remotely in our way for the politician's purposes of manipulation and control. The news media, whores for the competition of the stations, is reduced to reporting not necessarily newsworthy items (those things that the American public needs, to help keep them informed citizens capable of making mature decisions), but saleable items. These are things that sell, that sell their station and the products of their promoters. Because newsworthy items are not always spectacular and dramatic what we often get are sensationalistic items blown seriously out of proportion and rarely necessary for making mature decisions as citizens of the USA.

In Barry Glassner's book entitled *The Culture of Fear*, he attempts to answer the questions, "Why are so many fears in the air and so many of them unfounded?" He reports that as crime rates plunged during the 1990s, two thirds of Americans *believed* they were soaring. Specifically, crime in Detroit went down by 20%, but the increased media *coverage* of violent crimes *increased* 600%. So if you watch TV and the nightly news, you might be led to believe that every tenth second someone is committing a violent crime and it is unsafe for you to go outside your house, when actually there are *fewer* crimes. Where does the responsibility lie? Can you and I hope to change the system? Yes, and no. We cannot attack the system, we are the system. We can only hope to change it from within. One person by one potential consumer. What if you, as a concerned citizen, stopped watching the news until there was something newsworthy being reported (could be a few years). What if you never read the articles in the paper that catered to the need to feed on bizarre and sick incidences of human behavior taken out of context? What power would they have over you? What if you voted for people who based their campaign on legitimate concerns that we as regular people have? What if you saw your doctor as an equal, capable of making mistakes and seeing the world through his/her own perceptions, those of the traditional medical model: pathologies, surgeries and drugs? You could consider their opinions and realize they are just that, opinions. You could reclaim your own power, knowing that each of us has our specialties, but we are all souls alike.

One of the things I pick up vibrationally when I visit big cities, several in particular, is the energy of competition. It spurs people to do well and it also creates heart attacks. It is an underlying energy that, once you get there, you enter what everyone jokingly refers to as the 'rat race'. The basis of competition is fear; fear of being left behind, in your career, in your community, financially, being embarrassed and humiliated if someone passes you over at the job, or of someone else's kid getting the star quarterback position. It drives people beyond their comfort zone financially and physically, leading to disease and unrest on many levels. No one is directly to blame, we create our own unique reality. But what about the consensus reality we are all sharing, the US of A? Can we step back enough to look at our own lives to see what is truly important and what the mass vibration of fear drives?

When I was a master's student studying at the Monterey Institute to be a diplomat or a CIA agent, I worked in the library so that I could stay informed about everything in every country of the world. I knew the foreign service exams were coming up and I had to know who was the leader of every country, what was going on and how the US stood on it (all of which changed every other day). I read magazines in French, newspapers in German, articles in Russian, and news broadcasts from Britain. I knew everything that was happening politically from Chad, Africa to Novosibirsk, Soviet Union and everywhere in between. Then one day it occurred to me. I hadn't the foggiest idea what was going on inside of *me*. I didn't have a deep or meaningful relationship with anyone (I didn't have time) and didn't know how *I* stood on anything. What a humbling realization. It coincided with my decision to withdraw my application from the CIA and I subsequently stopped reading anything socially newsworthy for many years. I vowed to know and change *me* for the better, and thought somehow that was a nobler goal, changing the world by one person.

I have heard from several patients of my husband who have been diagnosed with heart sensitivities or high blood pressure that if they do only one thing; stop watching the nightly news, their pressure drops and they have significant positive mood changes. Certainly something to consider, and realize we have more choices than we are led to believe we do. So in assessing our emotional baggage, stepping away from being informationally overstimulated can help us find a clearer path to what is really ours.

KARMIC ISSUES

Lastly, I want to explore the idea that each of us comes prepackaged, with our own set of attributes and propensities, de-

pending upon the karma we need to work out. I liken it to select-
ing courses for a college year. As we are making decisions about
coming into an incarnate self, we have a class schedule listing
every possible option for learning. There are some classes we need
to take, offered only every so often, for our major, some we need
to take for our general education classes and then some we want
to take. Then, if we are adventurous, we may sign up for an elec-
tive, club or choir if we have time. Depending upon the semester,
we may do some volunteer work, get a part time job or join a
sorority. What seems to happen, in college as in life, is that we get
overwhelmed. We have to drop a class or extracurricular activity,
then lessen our workload, until we can handle the semester. Some
classes are a lot harder than what we expected. I suggest that we
come with our course plan in mind. Then we choose particular
physical/emotional/spiritual/mental attributes that lend themselves
to this learning project. I even think that those who commit suicide are ones who have to drop out of college altogether, they do
not feel prepared or cannot find the assistance they allocated for
this incredible learning project. They have to go back, regroup
and either try it again, or choose another possibility. But here we
are, with the set of parents, color of hair, IQ, height, geographical
location and so on that prepare us for the particular journey created just *for* us, *by* us.

These attributes aren't created by coincidence either, I suspect. They are picked from the gardens we have planted. Previous
to who we are now, we have been having experiences, positive and
negative, making decisions, giving and taking, making assessments
of life wherever we are. We were sowing seeds that we are now
reaping. It isn't just about repaying negative debts either. If you
spent a whole life giving to others at the exclusion of yourself, the
universe has a debt to repay to you in the giving department. It is
the balance of the universe. Some people believe that a negative
deed brings the repayment back tenfold, but I believe that im-

putes judgment, and I don't see that the universe judges. It only balances.

I don't expect all of you to believe this. That is not important. What is important is to allow for some responsibility to go to the participant, that what may seem like it needs or requires changing to you, the spouse or parent or child, was custom-made for that person for some potentially powerful awareness or learning.

For example, if you had beliefs that women are inferior beings and men hold the key to managing life properly it would stand to reason that you might choose to incarnate in a family that upholds these views. You may find yourself in a family belonging to a religious sect that forbids women many choices and are always subjugated to men. It will either allow you to continue on this particular path, or faced by the blatant misuse of power, this community will be more than your soul can stand and thus will act as a springboard for you to move beyond the reality created by this imbalanced belief.

8 War Games

One of the fundamental dynamics of relationships is that of conflict and war. I sometimes think it is an integral part of the Earth School, perhaps the common denominator of all of us here on this planet. I am not speaking of war in the context solely of Spartan type, aggressive, male, combatant, country-to-country killing and maiming, although it includes that. I am talking about war as in "a struggle between opposing forces or for a particular end." Your first reaction may be, "Well, not me, I am a pacifist or I really don't like conflict or elicit it." I have thought a lot about this concept of a struggle for a particular end that most always comes with an opposing force. The more I put things in this model, the more I see that fits.

Let's start with one person. How can one person have a war? There can be a struggle between two sides of a person, between the top half and the bottom. Between various parts of a person, between the spiritual and the physical, between the ego and the mental, between the thighs and the buttocks, the back and the brain, a part of us we deem defective and the rest of the body that is functioning normally. Some of you may understand right away what I am talking about, you live with it daily, but for the rest, let me make it clearer. Think of that part of your body you have previously identified as your weak spot. Everyone has one, it is where you store your stress, or where you start to hurt first in times of stress. It is your stress indicator. How do you feel about that part of you, your lower back or neck or knees, whatever it is for you? Do you feel integrated and fond of this part of you? Usually not. Usually you feel disappointed and let down by it too often. This is the beginning of a struggle. As life continues and your identified weak spot takes the brunt of most of life's stressful times, you increase your intolerance for this dang body part. You consult someone about removing it or performing surgery on it, or drugging it out of earshot. The little war escalates. Life moves on. You stuff more and more into your weak spot and since you have energetically identified it as your weak area it, in essence, becomes your weak area. Now it gives you more trouble sooner in response to stress, plus you are getting older and your natural elasticity and tolerances are growing thinner. You find some way to silence it (drugs or surgery), but it only seems to become more aggravated. Expecting your back to go out when you need it most, you aren't surprised when it does. You don't have kind things to say about it in return and never think about your back positively. You have waged a full-scale war.

Now look what happens next, energetically. You used to have a stress detector, something that humans are born with, and that comes in very handy to alert us when we step outside our comfort zone. Now you have an enemy. You dislike that part of you, your lower back or feet or whatever. The enemy lives within you. That doesn't stop it from being an enemy, and when you energetically declare someone or something as an enemy, you send it negative energy. When you send something negative energy, it receives it. It applies laws of the Universe to that energy, and says it will return that energy in kind. Now *you* are the enemy of it! Do you see how this works? When you attack or project negative feelings, thoughts, words, or swords, or guns, the natural propensity of most all living things is to fight back, to return the same energy sent. I am sure you have all seen this in life many times. Think about your boss or your child. When you speak to them with aggression and anger, what do you get? Much of the same volleyed back. When you begin your conversation with the energy of love and community, they feel that as well and respond. Don't you remember your grandmother ever saying, "You get more with honey than with vinegar?" Same idea.

I could spend the whole chapter on one person. There are not only physical parts of us we war against, there is our spiritual side, our mental side, our emotional side and so on. Ever get mad at yourself for being overly emotional or not responding with enough emotion? Ever try to stop your mind from thinking, to meditate in a calm space of no-thoughts? You will want to kill your own brain if you truly expect the brain to stop thinking thoughts. That's what it *does,* it thinks. Are there personality attributes that fall into the category of enemy also, facial expressions that remind you of someone you don't care to emulate? I even know people who specialize in soul retrieval, insinuating that we can be at odds and separated from parts of our own divine soul. We are but one person, yet we can have as many wars inside us as we permit. As I said earlier, I think this is part of the human incarnation journey, so don't kick yourself for not feeling whole and integrated.

THE WORLD AT WAR

Now let me glance at our personal world. What wars do we have? Still not certain there are any in your life? What about with your spouse or significant other, your mother or daughter? What is that definition we are working with again? *A struggle between opposing forces or for a particular end.* It's not like our spouse is an opposing force, well, not all the time, but there is usually always a struggle for a particular end. Take one day in the life of two people. When are you in total agreement with everything that other person wants to do? Try spending the day with someone, every second of that day. You will consciously or unconsciously want things your way. This café, not that one; this table, not that one; this temperature for the interior of the car, not too hot; this direction to move through traffic; this street or parking spot or alleyway or whatever it is. It is the nature of humans to have wills. There is nothing wrong with that. But if we are to engage in the relationship game, and hope to advance our pieces around the board, we must understand the rules. There are wills. Where there are wills, there is war. As I continue to give you more examples of our world at war, I will also bring light on how you can live life with fewer struggles. How you can cease engaging the enemy and *integrate*, instead of alert, the opposing forces. By their very nature, then, they will no longer be *opposing* forces.

Let's see. The fight against cancer, the war on drugs, the antibiotics fighting the bacteria, the antihistamines fighting the body's natural mechanism of draining the nasal passages, the flu vaccines attacking the flu, aspirins struggling against fevers, doctors righteously fighting against premature death. More? Yes, antiperspirants attacking sweat glands, the pancreas struggling with the amounts of sugar our western world consumes. One sports team fanatic squared off against another, one sport versus another, even conflicts between participants in the same sport (down hill skiers versus cross country skiers, and cross country versus snowmobilers, and snowmobilers avidly against the ecologists on and on). Not to mention the ongoing battle of whites against blacks or yellows against reds or communists against capitalists or Catholics against Muslims. Women against men, children against adults, poor against the rich, intelligent against the uneducated, state against state, country against country.

Now, can you honestly say you live without war? Can you even get up in the morning and go five minutes without engaging in some kind of struggle? Trying to straighten curly hair, curl straight hair, stop sweat from happening, struggle against age spots with anti-aging cremes. Maybe it is the nature of being human, but what if we are Divine, like I believe we are, can we rise above our humanness, into Divineness? I would like to think so, otherwise we may never graduate from this Earth School.

We are bombarded everyday in the newspapers, on television and the radio with all sorts of fights. The struggle against getting old, or sagging breasts, the fight against leukemia, or multiple sclerosis. Lawyers base their entire careers on one fight versus another. Marketing has made a science of finding our Hatfields and McCoys. Do you want to be embarrassed with psoriasis or get high cholesterol? Then take this medication that will fight those things for you. Do you want to look poor or uneducated? Buy these clothing lines that project a more desired outcome and surpass the Joneses. Do you want to look outdated, god forbid, and lose your advantage? No, you want to win, to get that job promotion or handsome date. It is a war out there. Win or lose, better make the right decisions. It's a dog-eat-dog world. No wonder we are all on the verge of a nervous breakdown.

Then once you get to work, if you can get dressed and showered without too much conflict, it is your company competing against another company, your department against another department, or you against a fellow employee. If you make it home without losing your place in line, fighting traffic, getting through the rat race, you could try to relax. You may even have an evening without your weak spot battling you, but then find the neighbor struggling with you because you made too much noise last night or forgot to return his electric turkey slicer and it's October and he will need it soon. Not only is it wills against wills, it is egos against egos, beliefs against beliefs, colors versus colors, teams versus teams, players versus players. It is so much the nature of our human incarnation you may be wondering why I am bringing it up. "Yeah, we breathe air, so what?"

I bring it up because this very nature, natural or created, is undermining every relationship we have, from the ones we have with ourselves to the ones we have with foreign countries. When we sit and arrogantly judge our political administration for playing war with other countries the way little boys play with toy soldiers, are we really any different, at any level? We are not so blatant, that is for sure, but can we say we are above war? When we engage in the struggle of light versus darkness, evil versus goodness, God versus Satan, are we any different than those politicians playing with miniature armies on the front lawn? As long as we are engaged in something versus the other, we are creating a negative relationship, we are empowering an enemy.

Many times it is those we love the most who we make our enemies, refusing to give in to someone else's will or fixedly determined to have it our way. As long as we identify something that we are against, whether it is our aching lower back or that annoying Middle Eastern country, we are creating through our very thoughts and energy, an enemy. As we have witnessed in this country, when we actively engage in warfare with another country, they retaliate, to whatever level they are capable. They may have been totally ignoring us as a nation until we turn our negative vision and physical attention on them. It's no different with bees or wasps. Leave them alone, and more than likely they won't be any problem for you. Go moving their nests and you have another situation altogether. I am not suggesting that you cease to have opinions. There is another possibility. Think about this. Have opinions, but know that they are just that, opinions. What is the definition of opinion, anyway? Webster's has two equally poignant ones: "1) a belief stronger than impression and less strong than positive knowledge and 2) judgment." If something were a judgment, I would venture to say it is also pretty personal. If it were personal, why would you assume that others would have the same one as you? I am not here to argue that opinions are personal, and also emotionally charged. I mostly want to get to the root of relationships again.

Putting opinions and personal will aside for a moment, let's look at my premise about relationships, that there is a reason for each one, remember? If we battle everything and everyone, how can we effectively know which battles are specifically, karmically ours? When we are constantly being ignited all day, which ones are there as teachers to take us through old healing to find our highest selves, and which ones are there to get us to make more purchases?

What if we could *integrate* instead of *segregate*? What if we could resolve differences or struggles by *accepting* the other instead of *rejecting* them? Let's try an example. Let's look at our chronic lower-back pain person. First, we must extinguish the idea of two sides. There are no rival teams. The back begins to hurt, the person gets annoyed. That is day one, no war has been declared yet. Instead of ignoring the significance in your own life — lower-back pain is pretty personal — you make a friend of the pain. Pull it in to your inner team, if you must have a team. Speak to it, console it, seek to understand it. There is a reason right now for the lower back pain. It has not yet become the energetic dump station of the body, it is just a messenger. It may be saying something as simple as you had better get a little more fit or stop straining so hard while gardening. It is a very practical message, perfect for you at this time of your life. But who wants to hear from their back that they need to trim up? It may be saying things that have to do with support. Lower back pain quite often equals support issues, such as worrying about finances or core living issues like raises and bonuses and child support and insurance checks and mortgage payments. Your back is saying, "I don't like what is going on right now." You may feel the back is being redundant since you would easily concur, but the pain in the lower back is actually providing a stimulus for something, usually change. This is where we want to declare war. But let's stop here, let's assume you are worried about financial issues you believe are out of your control. You spend the evening with the lower back. You explore options, you let your inner self tell you things, and you give your brain the night off. It is between you and your back.

Often I talk to my plants while gardening or pruning my flower gardens and was surprised a few years ago as they talked back. I was verbally abusive about one of my coworkers who happened to be my boss, in title only, not in the structure of the company and I was feeling hamstrung and annoyed by him. I didn't figure it would do any harm to let off some steam while gardening during my lunch hour. I was lucky enough to walk to work and could meander home for lunch if the weather permitted. I heard my tomato plants reply that I should forgive this man for his annoying behavior. I said, "Forgive him? Why would you say that?" They responded that I had forgiven my brother the year before because of their suggestion and it had worked out wonderfully. I remembered that it had. I said, "Hey, you guys are totally different tomatoes, how can you know about last year? I had varieties that did not reproduce and you couldn't even be from their seed." I didn't really get a complete metaphysical answer on the nature of tomato knowledge, but I felt certain they were simply accessing organic wisdom. That's what I am suggesting you do. Remember that organic wisdom is an inherent pool of knowledge in the Universe and that it is free for everyone to access.

The idea is that you do not engage in negative energy, as children do in name-calling, either with yourself or someone else. Reflect on the things in your life you think poorly of, or negatively about. Is it the annoying mosquitoes buzzing around your ear, the termites taking over the underside of your house, aphids building cities in your garden roses, or woodpeckers attacking your expensive wooden siding? We all have a number of them,

things or people or creatures that constantly challenge us. We begin each encounter with them in a defensive posture, ready for a
fight.

Did you ever see one of those photocopier jokes pasted above
the company copy machine that says something to the effect that
"the harder your day is going the more the copier will jam, and
the more you are in a hurry, the more it will break down"? I used
to laugh at that while copying, knowing deep inside me that it
wasn't really that far from the actual truth, but couldn't figure out
why. Really, as odd as I may seem, talking to plants and reading
nonvisual energy, I still did not believe inanimate objects had a
soul or a purpose for breaking the backs of humans. Now I understand it perfectly as the law of energetic response. The energy
we send out is what we receive in return.

When you are having a rough day, and we all have them,
things only seem to get worse as the day goes on until you hear
yourself saying, "Well, of course, I could have figured *that* was
going to happen, with a day like today has been." Most of the
jobs I have ever had entailed working with people, and I have
noticed on more than one occasion the response of other people
to someone in a bad or irritable mood. I once worked next to a
woman who, over the phone, assisted people with their broad-
cast-video needs and questions. Calls would come in and ran-
domly (or not?) would go to whichever support person was available. It never failed though, when she was in a grouchy mood, she
invariably would get the most challenging customers. I could hear
her break out into a serious argument with a client and end up
getting really upset. I always wondered why I hadn't gotten that
call, I may have been more prepared, and could have handled the
client in a completely different way. But the calls I got were up-
beat and without much or any conflict. It happened enough times
for me to realize it is our own energy attracting like energy, as
effortlessly as a bee to honey.

As you can see, I am not considering the *victim card* as an option. I don't think some people are born with a propensity to hard luck or negative experiences. I *do* however think that people are born with propensities to certain kinds of energy, and unbeknownst to them attract more of the same.

ENERGETICALLY ENGAGING THE ENEMY

Let me give you another example of the fight we engage in on a daily basis. You are a typical American and so sit down to watch a bit of television after work to relax. The commercials that litter the program tell you, and you're probably not really listening, so they go directly into your subconscious, that it is cold and flu season. Do they tell you this informatively? No, they don't pretend to be the news. They tell you this because they sell a product that fights the cold and flu. They are telling you to prepare yourself for the yearly battle of colds and flus that we, as humans, must invariably get at this changing weather time of the year. Brace yourself for the fight. You know they are coming, get your weapons and prepare for battle. Once I started paying attention to how many places tell us it is cold and flu season, I began to notice how, with clockwork precision everyone starts coughing and sniffling as if on cue. I even saw one sign in a doctor's waiting room say, "It's *almost* cold and flu season." They are getting you ready to get ready!

Which came first, the chicken or the egg? Are they correct? Is it inevitably cold and flu season and there is nothing we can do about it, or are we beginning a fight that needn't ever be fought? Are we predestined to have a cold every year? Personally, I don't think so. I think that we begin the energy of attack. According to my model, what does that action elicit? The same action coming back. I have a running joke with my next-door neighbor who gets a flu shot every year and then comes down with the flu the following week. I always laugh, along with her skeptical husband, that she just went and *got* the flu. She assures me that her flu episode would have been much worse without the shot. Maybe so, who is to say? I just come from another perspective, the energy one. The flu, like the wasps we referred to earlier, was minding its own business, doing what the flu does, expanding, mutating, thriving on weak individuals, dying out in others. Then along comes Betty, sword in hand, swinging and flailing, calling out, "You evil flu, be gone with you, I call upon you to stay away from me, and die an untimely death!" The flu looks up from what it is doing and goes, "Whoa, Betty over there looks yummy, why I never even noticed her before she started yelling at me." Basically, it is energy begetting energy, positive or negative. We begin a fight, what we get back is a fight of equal intensity.

I remember several years ago a story in the news about a young girl who was kidnapped and then killed. I thought it was a terrible story, so difficult for us to hear about tragedies to children, and when I read the details found out that the little girl's mother had made her practice being abducted many times during her short childhood. She knew exactly what to do, how to kick and scream and yell for help and all the things one would learn while training for this kind of event. I wondered about that energetically. I am not trying to insinuate the mother created it through her training and obsession with being abducted. I just wonder, why her? Of all the children in the world, why her? What was it about her energy that her mother picked up and tried intuitively to counter, like a fairy would try to undo an evil curse? These things make me ponder the infinitely complex nature of karma.

Now that you may be willing to admit that our world is more fraught with war than you would like to admit, what can we do about any of it? I am not going to insist you stop watching television and listening to the news or reading the paper, but it actually might be a good idea. I am going to offer, along with the simple eye opening awareness that it is happening, some suggestions for avoiding the fights. Simply not engaging is one way. Ever have an argument where someone doesn't argue back? It doesn't last very long. It may become a soliloquy, but it ceases to be a fight.

PUT YOUR SWORD DOWN

This is where I simply say, "*Put your sword down.*" Didn't Jesus of Nazareth say something awfully close to that? Okay, so it's not an original idea, it just never becomes obsolete. Take any example: the termites, the lower back, the aging hands, your mother-in-law, it is the same answer. Do not engage in a fight. Your ego may want you to, your newsman may tell you you have to, to be a good American, your ingrained response may take you there, but don't go. The ingrained response is going to be the biggest obstacle. We are brought up with this kind of "struggle between opposing forces" as our daily life material. I am suggesting we make it something other than that. I am not suggesting peace. That word has too many weak connotations. I am suggesting non-engagement and integration.

If you have ever studied the martial art, Aikido, you see how this art takes the concept I am speaking of and uses it as a form of actively rerouting intended aggression. The student or master of Aikido uses the flowing energy of the force of an attacker to swiftly squelch the incident by redirecting the attacker's own energy. For example, an angry brute is coming at you with his full force. You stand calmly in his way until the moment of apparent impact, but just a brief second before smashing heads, you step outside the line of attack and bring the pursuer's energy with you in a guided direction, redirecting the aggressive energy into a circle, or back upon himself. It is a very graceful and nonviolent method of diffusing angry energy and transforming it. Interestingly, Aikido was developed from the sword fighting methods of the Japanese samurai. It is a perfect example of a violent, aggressive method turned into one of defense and harmony.

Let's look at an unusual case I worked through with a woman from Northern California. Her lovely and expensive home had been eaten thoroughly once and was going on twice by a band of woodpeckers. She had spent thousands of dollars getting exterminators to rid her of these pests (the fight). They not only didn't go away, they dug in for helping number two after she had replaced the wood siding with fresh boards. She said the pieces of wood taken off looked more like lace than wood. She finally asked me to assist. I had never had any direct contact with woodpeckers, but believed in what I am telling you, stop the war. So I said I would see what we could do together. I connected with the woodpeckers, energetically, from another physical location and asked what was up. I asked what it would take for them to stop the wood siding munching, realizing of course that this is the nature of woodpeckers. What ensued, (I can feel this story getting a little too bizarre for most readers and the specific details would take up another book itself), is that the very day we talked and made peace and I promised them my client would stop sending men to spray them and kill them, they left. We connected in a way that allowed them to continue doing what they do in the nearby woods, without the risk of them and all their offspring being poisoned. They were seen around the area, but she never had woodpecker problems again. I suggested she create a relationship with them so that when she saw them she wouldn't say, "Those dang woodpeckers, they have cost me so much money, I hate them." She would say, "I have learned so much from those dang woodpeckers, that to cooperate, or meld, or connect on an *equal* level is where we live harmoniously" (edited for the family version).

Equality is the big word here. It isn't about placating or belittling or thinking that we are big superior humans and will cooperate with these lowly aphid creatures because it just might work and then they won't eat the roses. It is about honoring and cooperating with every living thing, because there is a reason for it in your life. Every living thing is here to teach and learn something.

If we are above every other creature's learning or teaching, we have missed out on a lot of wisdom.

Now let me get to human relationships, which is where I was heading with this war thing. I hope I have made a point about all the other small and not so small places we find to wage war. It is with other humans though that our greatest learning curve takes place. If we are in a constant state of defense or offense, preparing for war or waging it, how can we be open and receptive to our teachers? Remember the ones I talked about, as teachers or students, we are in relationships for a reason. It is about putting your weapons down first. Yes, it's true, you may get wounded, but I doubt it will be mortally. Someone has to start. If you are reading this book, it may as well be you, right?

Let's take your mother-in-law as an example. Maybe she annoys you and pushes all your buttons. In your protective nature toward your spouse, you get doubly irritated for the issues that bother him or her too. After many years of marriage and thus a relationship with this woman, you have a certain type of relationship set up. You prepare to see her, you put your armor on, you store biting comments close by in case you need them for retaliation. You brace yourself. I assure you, she is doing the same thing, strapping on her armaments and preparing for the worst of whatever may come. Let's say that one day you don't prepare yourself. It would be like not putting on your makeup. You are beautiful without it, but you aren't used to being seen this way. It unarms people. She comes over, takes a few preliminary shots, hits, but no retaliation. She may think she got through to a soft spot, she takes aim, strikes, hits again. Still no retaliation. Soon, the energetics of life say she will not persist. She is not getting the energetic feedback required to keep up the energy of attack. She desists. Next time you see each other, you may have a repeat, based on preprogramming, but the energetic attack will be extinguished faster. Soon what happens is that a new relationship takes the place of the fighting one. It may not be much of one at all, maybe all you had together was your mutual antagonism, but it is certainly going to be different, it can't help but be. Now, you can determine whether you have something to work out with this person, soul to soul, or was that just it? But you had to be the one to put your sword down first. What do you have to lose? Maybe a relationship, that's what. Some people say any relationship is better than no relationship, no matter how dysfunctional. If that is your opinion, I honor that and say, there is still something to learn, but why not graduate and learn the higher lesson? We all get it eventually anyway.

The battlefields that we fight on home territory are with the ones we love most. Most of the time, we are not prepared, we don't always strap on our arsenal, or maybe we are wearing it 24/7 and we aren't even aware of it. Either way, we are going to be attracting that with which we most resonate.

Here I need to interject an energy understanding concept. Let's say that you, on a given day, are feeling mildly angry, not full blown, seeing red, number ten angry, but maybe a four on a scale of 0-10. The negative, angry thoughts you are thinking are electric waves that are plugging in to every other "Number-Four Angry-Person" in the Universe. You have just plugged your energy into *everything* that vibrates on the same frequency of mild anger. The same goes with positive energy, which is the whole point of this. If you are resonating with a Number-Eight Gratitude, guess what? You just plugged into everything in the Universe that resonates with strong gratitude. Nice, huh? Gives you a boost, makes you feel high, connected, supported by the Universe, extremely capable. The corollary of that is that plugging into the negative does the same, non-judgmentally, simply giving you more of what you choose to resonate with. It's like my coworker on an irritable day, now is it any wonder she would draw the customers who are having an irritable day also? No, makes total sense energetically.

Let me give you another example. Ted is worried. He is worried that his company will be audited, that the companies he deals with will stop using his services, that he will eventually go bank-rupt. He has a reputable company, never cheats on his taxes and offers a fair deal. He worries anyway. Every little thing in the news looks like an indication of impending doom for his company. Every client that doesn't come in for several months is another indication that he is slowly going out of business, even though his monthly figures stay relatively constant. What is up for Ted? Well, if he continues to generate the vibration of worrying, he, in fact, will find much to worry about. He is sending out a beacon of energy much like a lighthouse, alerting all that similar energy to find haven here. Already, he is noticing what he worries about most is beginning to happen. Third party insurance companies are steadily decreasing benefits that cover his type of health ser-vice. He is going to worry himself out of a profession pretty soon. On the energetic side, he may be hearing internal messages, ones saying he is ready to move on, into some other kind of livelihood, or some other way of doing it.

What I am saying is twofold. One, there is a *reason* for the emotions we feel. Two, if we don't grasp the reasons and act upon them, they will generate an altogether different reality, one gener-ated by the unconscious and it's unlikely that it is the place our conscious selves would like to go. The journey is the same. It's just whether or not you want to spend a lifetime in suffering and conflict before you understand your internal messages and are able and courageous enough to act upon them. I see it like this, if we don't act on our negative internal messages, we attract every-one and everything that are also dealing with those same issues (like a huge group therapy session or the blind leading the blind) until we are forced to see ourselves, even if it is in someone else's mirror.

Returning to our loved ones and war, when we make some-one or something that someone does an enemy, we have declared an energetic war. That means, like in Spartan-type wars, you pre-pare offensively and defensively. Most likely, unless you consciously raise your vibration and don't act unconsciously, you are going to respond to the aggressive energy with equal or more intense aggression. In this time of split marriages and stepchildren, the war at home can be quite challenging and complicated. Have you declared war on the child or on the ex-spouse of your partner? Do they resemble each other enough in personality traits that soon you can't tell the difference between them? Does your own spouse cross invisible boundaries you have drawn in the sand, declaring an unspoken war as he/she does it? Are we allowing our own internal frustrations with work, life, romance to affect our relationship with everyone? Because that is what I am suggesting. What you resonate with is what you will attract. If you come home from work Number-Eight Angry and Number-Seven Frustrated and Number-Eight Resentful, you have preselected the evening's programming for all who enter your viewing arena. Is this how you want to spend your evening, watching anger, frustration and resentment? I can't imagine anyone who would consciously choose this channel.

UNPLUG FROM UNWANTED PROGRAMMING

Step back. Unplug from anger, resentment and frustration. How do you do this? Sure, if I could do that, I would have a different life. Exactly. Two things need to happen. One, accept that there are reasons, as I have alluded to, for these emotions. Do not ignore them, but realize they are for you, and not for everyone in your life. So usually, before you can deal with them, you have to get yourself into a spot where you are *able* to. At the back of this book is a list of negative emotions, there for singling out the specific emotions you are feeling so you can isolate the challenges. (See Managing an Emotional Word List in chapter nine). We will return to what to do about them. Second, but it may be first in actual chronological order, find another, more positive vibration to replace anger, resentment and frustration (or whatever yours are). This will set you up for resonating with the vibrations that will assist instead of detract. For example, if you are trying to get out of anger, or understand why it is in your life, you won't be able to come up with any other possibilities other than anger as long as you are firmly resonating with its intense frequency.

GRATITUDE

This is my suggestion; choose the feeling of gratitude. Replace with gratitude whatever negative emotions are plaguing you. Many people say that in extreme negative situations there doesn't seem to be a thing in the world to be grateful for. I suggest you have something ready beforehand (instead of snide comments). Choose a few things you are genuinely grateful for while you are in a grateful mood. Store them in your handy nearby mental container for recalling when you need to take yourself out of a negative space into a positive one. Keep your little gratitude stash close by, ready for use. When you begin to become consumed by a negative emotion or emotions either just *feel* what they are or try to find them by consulting the emotional word list at the back of the book. Now, first and foremost, acknowledge that you are feeling whatever it is. That is saying, I am going to deal with you, I see you there and recognize something is askew. It is like bookmarking the emotion, intending to come back to it.

One of two things will then happen assuming you are capable of really manifesting the gratitude to change your vibration. Either you will find that the emotion wasn't actually yours (for example, it was a response marketed to you or sponsored by our society), and it will dissipate and leave you with your own genuine feelings about the subject. Or you will need to look at the source of this anger or frustration yourself. It has plagued you for a while anyway and now needs to be given proper attention. Give some respect to why your energy system would generate these intense emotions for you. You are calling a truce long enough to know why you are at war with someone or something. Then you can eventually make a peace treaty. As you look 360 degrees around your life, you can now see where you have been making scrimmages and blitzkriegs and little wars all over the place, and quietly, honorably, lay your weapons down. You will not lose, as is our innate fear in dropping our weapons. No, in fact, you will gain, because that is what everyone's human lesson takes them through. The sooner you see through the illusion of struggle within the human incarnation, the sooner you graduate. Graduation is simply taking you to a higher plane, a higher vibration, closer to your highest self. One of your tools now, *gratitude*, is there to help you make it through some difficult spots, hopefully enough to turn the tide in the battle.

WELCOME THE MESSAGE

That being said, how do you lay down your sword and welcome the message without killing the messenger? It is as simple, or as impossible, as looking at the world through a different pair of viewing lenses. Instead of seeing everything that is annoying or uncomfortable as an opportunity for conflict, no matter how small, try to see it as a message sent especially for you, no matter how small. This may sound vain or conceited. How can everything that happens have a purpose for *me*? Well, it *is* happening to you, that much is personal. You *are* responding to it in a personal way, it *is* personal. So what if it is national policy that is annoying you the most right now, it is still personal in how you respond to it.

We need another example. I want to use enough examples that you feel pretty sure that you can apply these concepts to your own life. Let's take an easy one. I won't start with America's foreign policy. Imagine that you want to make a pumpkin soufflé for your sweetie as a special dessert treat. You begin with all the ingredients and a positive attitude, even though you have never actually made a soufflé before. You slap in all the items on the recipe list, stir and bake. Well, it's not rising, it's not doing it's puffy thing, and the longer you look in the oven, the less it looks like a soufflé. It looks like pudding, if you use your imagination. At this point instead of getting irritated and swearing off baking specialty items, you think, what can I do with what I have? How can I *integrate* what I already have into what I want? Without starting all over, there is no longer time for that, you take your pumpkin delight and let the smell and texture tell you what it's capable of being. Or you figure it out with your big brain, I prefer the former, since my big brain doesn't have as many creative ideas. Your pumpkin soufflé wanna-be is now the crème filling for a boxed spice cake with caramel icing. Wow! Who would've thought of that? No harm done and no war. Integration. Melding. Cooperation. And maybe that was the message your soul was trying to communicate today, "Honey, you need to be a little more flexible if we are going to be able to change and grow and bend into what you dream of being." See how this works?

Here is an example that includes creature relations, saving *human* relations for last. Everyone has pests that bother them, whether they are bugs or animals or insects. Flies are something everyone should be able to identify with. My husband says that flies are what gave bugs their name, they *bug* you. You may be thinking ahead, wondering and musing about how a fly can have a message for you. Let your creative self help you find the answers. Flies actually have many purposes in the evolution of humans. Really. First, they are annoying to most humans, they make irritating sounds and fly in chaotic directions. You can't swat them too easily because of this unique feature they have of being able to take off in any direction, and it is embarrassing flailing the swatter around with no consequence. So, they assist in helping the human involved to concentrate. They provide the stimulation for centering and concentrating. It's as if, when they show up in your quiet room, they were sent there by your Zen master to see if you can focus on what you are doing with this intensely annoying sound and distracting movement. They also, like all creatures, provide an opportunity to connect. As strange as this may seem, I have identified flies, especially the big black kind, as sentinels for dark energy while I am working. They alert me, when dark energy has shown up in my energy healing session, that I should scan my working area for unwanted visitors that may try to sabotage the work. These fly sentinels have proven seriously helpful on many occasions. So, in order to thank them, I volunteer to take them outside without hurting them. This can be pretty difficult if they don't cooperate. Finally, I speak mentally to them saying that if they will trust me, and I try not to hurt them to the best of my human ability, by landing on my hand I will know they want out. It's like training a puppy to scratch at the door when they need to go out and relieve themselves. The first time I tried this I wasn't sure how it would work, but on many occasions my helpful visitor would sit right on my hand and wait. I would stop what I was doing and put it safely outside. It has been an odd experience for many a client.

Once again, put the fly swatter down, look at what you were doing before the fly distracted you. Was there something you were thinking about that a part of you is trying to sabotage, to stop a dream from coming true? Were you thinking about something that you *should* be distracted from, to keep you from going down that road of negativity? When we allow our energy to vibrate with chaotic, annoying energy, we are not very centered and focused on what we are doing. The key is in being creative, allowing in an alternative solution to a previously decided irritating situation. Try it. You can always speak to any being's higher self and if they are connected to the rest of the Universe, they will hear.

What about human relations? Why is that so trying? Because you don't have the option of swatting them with a fly swatter or throwing them in the trash if they come out of the oven looking like pudding instead of soufflé? Maybe, but more than likely because they have a will oftentimes equal to your own. This means the fight is often grander.

Let's take an example. How about a husband and wife (substitute what works for you)? Tom, the husband, and Gerry, the wife, have a pretty happy relationship. The only thing that gets Gerry going is when Tom forgets to put the toothpaste lid on the toothpaste, but she has begun to overlook that. What really bugs her, without her consciously being aware of it, is when he insinuates with innocuous comments that she is not capable of being a leader, of making decisions herself. He doesn't mean to belittle her, he simply assumes that she knows this factual information about herself. She often waits for someone else to make a decision, and thus does not inspire confidence of leadership. So, one day they are discussing plans for building a new house and Gerry decides she wants to be in charge of the day-to-day supervision of the construction crew. Tom, scoffing, says something to the effect that too many mistakes would get through and she would have to wait till he got home to ask him anyway. Gerry feels her face getting red (signals of Level One Alert) and arms herself with attack rifles, ready to shoot him down, prove him wrong. Let's stop the scene here. We can see, as the viewing audience, why she is getting riled up. It is a core issue for her and she is trying to find her own voice and command authority with it. She has been getting increasingly upset over issues of her apparent impotence and powerlessness in her existing world. Tom is naturally challenging it, as either the springboard for that voice, or the status quo keeper, whichever Gerry chooses. He is probably not conscious of that, but plays the role nonetheless.

What does Gerry do to vent the steam, to redirect her brewing anger? Stop, put the weapon down, unarm. Do not lash out at the message boy. If you were Gerry, you could ask yourself, "Why am I getting hot behind the collar here?" It will be a little harder to see your own issues than someone else's that are clearly written on their forehead. Remember, Gerry, Tom's only experience with you over the past 12 years has been subservience and acquies-cence. Why would he think anything has changed? Good point. Know that he is challenging your own fears, can I really be in charge of men building my own house, and why shouldn't I have that right? Will I be honored or walked over? Tom doesn't know, but you know he is lighting up the issues. Wow, thanks Tom, for shining that much needed flashlight on my fears and issues. Once you see through the illusion of the battle, you see there needn't be a battle at all, you received the message and will try very hard to be fair and confident while dealing with the construction team building your home. Know that each interaction or challenge you have while on the construction site is also challenging your fears and issues. Don't yell at the electrician, apply the rules of self-analysis. Don't chew out the plumber, know that it is a perfect Universe and what is happening is happening for a purpose, ex-pressly for you (and the plumber). It isn't your responsibility to see that the plumber gets *his* message, only that you see yours. Thank Tom for kindly showing you that you are engaged in build-ing your own confidence and would appreciate his patience and support. He probably will respond a lot better than screaming and escalating to Level Three Alert.

If I could outline a set of suggestions for you while disarming, it would be:

1) Pay attention to the emotion/emotions coming through your energy system. Bookmark them and go to number two.
2) Take a deep breath and pull the gratitude card out of your sleeve (changing your vibration).

3)   Now put on the glasses that allow you to see outside your
       small physical self, into your energetic self. Who is trying
       to say what to you? Why? Why now? How does it make
       sense? Why this emotion? Indulge in self-analysis. Listen
       to your little voices.

4)   Now meld, soften, cooperate, find a useful way to take
       this potentially explosive situation and turn it into a
       useful and positive experience. Integrate. Know that you
       are not that different from what was moments ago,
       almost your enemy. How are you the same? Why have
       you come into each other's lives?

No matter how small, try these questions. One by one, we
become part of the solution and cease contributing to the war
effort. We no longer prevent the Earth herself from graduating to
a higher level of occupants as well. When we are offered a higher
perspective, we find greater wisdom by viewing the bigger picture. What these tools and concepts offer are just that, a higher
perspective and hopefully the wisdom that accompanies it.

9 Creative Ideas and New Awarenesses

DARK NIGHT OF THE SOUL

As you are walking the journey we call life, even though you may try everything to remain positive, to connect with your extrasensory helpers and stay in compassion as much as you can, you still may find yourself in what I call a *cave process*. As in a real cave, everything feels dark and unknown and there doesn't appear to be any hope or light to direct you. Depression may set in and everything that you have heretofore known and liked no longer has the slightest appeal. Food you used to like doesn't give you any pleasure. People who ordinarily bring you a great deal of joy or delight now feel drab or dull. Even the clothes that always made you feel better don't do a thing for you. Colors, places, music, all are lost to your senses, because your senses have become dulled or even deadened. You went from living in the joy of light, hopefulness and community to a time of darkness and introversion. Some monks from the Middle Ages called this the Dark Night of the Soul. As painful as this process may seem at the time, it isn't necessarily a *bad* thing.

As you grow and change along your life path, either with someone else or alone, you ask and you receive, you face your fears, challenge them and overcome their power over you. Life feels in control. Synchronicity is really doing its thing. Offers are coming, experiences are opening up to you that seem like *just* what you needed at that precise moment. You feel like you are really flowing along in life's river, and it feels good. Then, pow, almost overnight, the lights go off. Where? Why? Who? What? No answers, no community, no thing. Just aloneness. Maybe you have never had this happen, but chances are if you are reading this book, you either have or will have one day. So stay tuned. Suddenly, all the certainty you had about what you are doing and who you have become and your connection to a nonphysical reality are hanging on by a thread. I see this time in one's life as a result of challenging a belief pattern too big to get through by the regular route. What if you needed to go, or better yet, were *asking* to go, somewhere that in order to get there, you had to either take a different vehicle or be a different person. What if you had to be a different molecular being to fit into the space you are presently asking to go? What then? Would an anonymous friend synchronistically send you a book about how to transform into another being? Would you meet someone who is an alchemist who is looking for a human subject? Maybe, but since you may already be so happy and content in the great space you're presently living, you would most likely lay the book aside for another time, and tell the alchemist he'd better not change anything for the worse, because life couldn't be better right now.

You're ready, you have mastered one certain reality and are now ready for a multidimensional reality. You have naturally guided yourself to something more fulfilling on more levels and more awesome in every way. You are ready to become aware of more of the universe, more dimensions, more universal truths from which you can draw more wisdom and add your unique signature. But you're too stuck in the material world, or rather the illusion of the material world. You have learned how to navigate pretty well through the buildings and spaces and walls of your world. What if where you want to go is closer to your highest self and that highest self has fewer boundaries? What if there aren't as many (or any) walls? What if you are only accessing one-tenth the information you *could*? What if you had to be transformed and for this to happen everything you believed in had to be destroyed and rebuilt? A cave might be a nice place for such an occurrence. Remember there are many seeds that can only germinate in the darkness. Imagine, before becoming a beautifully fragrant trumpet flower you have to get your roots set firmly in the dark, damp soil.

This is what is happening. You are getting new roots. You are being restructured. We all cling tenaciously to our old habits and beliefs because that is what we know, who we are, what we have come to identify as ourselves, so it feels even more torturous having these familiarities ripped coldly from our grasping fingers. The reason I bring this up is because after you begin to consciously do soul work, you inevitably go through a transformation process. Maybe not to this degree, or maybe worse, but your life begins to change nevertheless. Actually, that is what you're wanting anyway. We just want it in a different way, accompanied by music and lights and a banner!

Many of my repeat clients invariably call me and ask what I have done to them. It is this multidimensional change that is occurring. I try to explain it the best I can, but I don't see the process as a terrible thing. It feels to me like a gift (well, once you can look back on it in hindsight) and a privilege to be restructured. It means you are evolving. You can't stop the process anyway, even if you would want to. We are all evolving at a certain rate, but conscious soul work accelerates the process.

There is another concept I call the *comfortable chair* that each of us has, as I mentioned earlier. It is made up of the things with which you are most familiar; physically, emotionally, spiritually, and habitually. If your response to humiliation is recoiling or stinging words, that is your comfortable chair every time you are confronted with humiliation. It is as if you have had many lifetimes of repeating the same responses to the same stimuli. Every life has a big comfortable chair, it welcomes, beckons sit a while, take a break, rest.

For example, you have been conscious that a repeated theme for you in this life has been to create dependent relationships. Everything you do unconsciously supports in some way your need to be needed, even if it means disempowering another in the process. This is your comfortable chair. It feels right as rain to help others, to assist them even if it is at your own expense. Something propels you, or usually many repeated things, and you become aware that your need to be needed in this way is not honoring another's own personal process. It makes you take a look at your own motives for defining yourself as valuable by being needed. You suddenly know that you must move beyond this spot. You stand up, push yourself away from your comfortable chair and start taking baby steps away from that comfort zone. That is harder than it sounds. Every time life challenges you, your first thought is to run back to the chair, curl up in it, take on more clingy people who need you so that you feel safe, needed and comfortable.

The new path is unknown and untraveled. In fact, the way may seem so rough and overgrown that it does not appear to be there at all. How do I function in the cave and how do I get out without succumbing to the powers of the dark, which are definitely there in the cave too, by the way? Oh great, blind, albino, biting creatures and bats too?? Did someone say it was going to be easy? Perhaps someone did, but we humans didn't seem to be listening when that part was being offered.

So here we are, in the cave, depressed, unhappy, lacking luster in life, not really caring where we go from here, or even that we continue to exist, in many cases. Imagine you are a house and you are being rewired from 110 to 220 volts. Everything in the house that runs on electricity will have to be temporarily disconnected. In fact, there will be an unspecified amount of time where there will be many inconveniences, forcing the homeowners to find new ways of coping with old habits. Nothing will run smoothly in this modern house with no electricity. Eventually, when the rewiring is complete, the house is ready for a stronger current of electricity to flow through it, enabling it to be able to carry more, faster and more powerfully. It is very similar to that when you are being rewired for multiple dimensions. If you are wired for 3-D, that's as much as you are capable of. Expect down time as you upgrade to more dimensionality.

I work with many people after they have begun to question their world. This starts that soul work process I alluded to when growth points the only direction, but nothing seems to shine a way. Many look at life and question, "Is this all? I did everything I was told, I followed the rules the best I could according to the text of my particular religious sect, but life just doesn't feel full or right. Isn't there some great feeling you're supposed to have when God is happy with you for being good? Aren't you supposed to feel better about yourself than this?" Why so many unspoken longings and unanswered questions then? Is it any wonder that once we start the process of removing negative belief patterns and open the way to a more whole, joyful being that some of the reasons that the belief pattern fit in the first place are now all gone? My clients think I have pulled the last remnants of familiarity out from under them as a result of our work together, but they were already in the process of doing that themselves.

Given enough time, patience and trust, within weeks or years, eventually what resurfaces is a new *being*. Someone who has found their own intimate connection to the Creator, the Divine, the one responsible for this whole Universe thing. It all comes in just the right time and through the process that is uniquely their own. For some reason, this Dark Night of the Soul is about just that, finding out who we are, where we came from and what we are doing here. Having a relationship with the Divine is how those questions all get answered.

Keep in mind that even though everything may feel *turned off* during this upgrade phase, you are not alone. Your assistance will come in the most unlikely places at the most unlikely times, but not by coincidence. To the extent to which you can hear these nonphysical helpers, they are locked on to you and attempt to facilitate whatever you most need during this dark night process. To suggest you connect with them during this time period is somewhat naïve, because the last thing that feels possible is connecting with anything, much less something Divine. Simply know somewhere in your heart, you have *not* been left alone. Your germination process is being greatly honored.

There's not really much friends or loved ones can do for you while you are in your cave. Hopefully an explanation like I just offered will help, but I trust that everyone will find the healing they need in just the right time, so I will leave you to enjoy the cave, or look forward to it, or reminisce about it with new awarenesses.

BALANCING HORMONES

What I want to offer now are a few things that make soulful evolution a little more manageable. One has to do with the physical self. As we go through metamorphic spiritual and emotional changes, the physical hormonal system goes wacky. Envision a meter with a needle indicator. First the needle goes swinging all the way in one direction and then all the way in the other, that's wacky. I have found, after trying an assortment of creams, ointments and pills that the best way to quickly and efficiently regain hormonal balance is to work on the hormones directly. How do you do that? Trust me on this one, I have tried them all (except the synthetic hormones). I spent almost two years in what I assumed was normal perimenopausal activity. Even though I was in my early forties, I bled more than I didn't and was convinced I was going to run out of blood before I made it to menopause proper. I tried all the natural options from black cohosh and wild yam to teas and creams touting female regulation. After reading so much about estrogen and the abundance of esters in our society, and becoming paranoid to eat, drink out of plastic bottles or sit on synthetic carpeting, I then went to progesterone cream. I tried increasing my daily intake of organic soy products. You name it, I tried it. Nothing had any effect whatsoever. The bleeding, feelings of discomfort and irritation persisted. Finally one day, my dear husband said, "Why don't you just balance your hormones? You balance everything else." He had a very good point and from that day forward that is what I have been doing and with miraculous results. My period has been more regular than when I was 20. I wish I had discovered this 25 years ago!

Not only is balancing the hormones good for women and whatever menopausal, perimenopausal or premenstrual problems you uniquely have, it is great for children having a tantrum, or men who are stuck in a heavily testosterone mediated place looking for mature relief. It even has great results with your pets. Everyone has hormones and they are more important in our daily functioning than most of us realize. By balance, I do not insinuate that I have a scale that measures everyone in the middle. Balance is as unique as each one of us, so it is different for every person. After I started having such great results with my ultimate guinea pig, me, I had an opportunity to try my balancing trick on a child I was working with. His mother asked me if there was something I could do for him. He was being picked on by all the boys in his neighborhood and at school. He had been playing with the girls in his neighborhood for as long as they had lived there and played with dolls and other traditionally girl things. The mother didn't mind that he played with dolls, but only that he was being excluded from playing with the other boys. I really didn't think this was within the scope of my practice, but said I would check on this one thing. I pulled up his energy system and found that he was registering at about 80 percent estrogen on my hormone scale. I also checked to see what balance or normal was for him, personally. Optimum balance for him registered in the mid 50s on my self-created scale of hormones. I noted that he was out of balance for himself personally.

I am not a biochemist and don't propose to know the exact ratio of female versus male sex hormones needed in the body. My scale is based on the energetics of the body, and when I balance a person's hormones I trust that it is that person's body alone that knows what their optimal ratio is. The numbers are for my mind only. In reading about hormones over the last several years, I have found case studies of women who work together all seem to link their menstrual cycles up, with the hormones of each participant affecting the others. Anyway, I suspect that he linked up his own hormonal balance to the girls who were his playmates, who would naturally have more estrogen. Keep in mind that each individual has a balance of both estrogen and testosterone. There are many other hormones (progesterone, etc.), but for the purposes of my work, and balance, I stay with estrogen and testosterone, yin and yang.

I got a call from this boy's mother two days later saying that she didn't know what I had done, but he was all boy. What *had* I done to him? What I was helping him find was his own balance. I followed up with him for several weeks, did some more energy adjustments, but found that he remained balanced at about 54%

estrogen. That was balance for him. He still plays with the same toys and friends, but seems to be more in balance than before.

I also did some hormonal balancing with a young dancer/choreographer, and after our work, she reported that she was able to access more feminine poses and openings and generally express herself over a broader range of feelings. She was extremely happy in her improved dancing attributes as well as in her primary relationship.

More than propensities to male or female activities, this is how to keep our bodies and the correlating emotions in balance. Having your hormones in balance, as anyone who has ever suffered from premenstrual syndrome knows, can make the difference between functioning and being an emotional wreck. Children who are having an emotional tantrum without any apparent reason often are responding to growing changes in their own chemistry and balancing their hormones is like giving them a soft blanket and a cookie. It is nature's kind way to soothe growing pains. The ability to do this is as simple as focusing the mind.

Here's what you do. It is unbelievably easy. In your mind's eye, imagine the person you are assisting. If it is you, imagine yourself, and focus your energy on them (or you). You simply say (out loud or to yourself), *"I want to project the perfect amount of hormones into — your name, child's name, whoever — for balance and harmony."* Then hold that focus. You may feel something, like a filling up or flowing out, or nothing at all, but your vibratory focus is doing its work. Hold that image until you feel there is nothing more to do. It may take as little as a few seconds or as long as a minute. It depends on how out of balance and how receptive they are. I do it on myself about once a week to maintain balance unless I feel emotional stresses are stronger than usual.

The key is focusing. Try not to do two things at once, try not to be thinking negative thoughts about yourself or that person, like, "Take this, you evil deed doer." Try to send the energy in love and compassion. You don't need to specify the hormone being added or deleted, their or your nature will do the balancing. It does not have any negative effects if you cannot do it, or if you cannot focus. If you are trying to put someone out of balance intentionally, you most likely will not get permission energetically to access their system. It doesn't have *any* negative side effects and has immediate results. It is the power of the human to heal itself. That's one of those changes in beliefs that need to happen for us to evolve. It acts like the power of positive thinking. Focusing positive energy on one part of a person for the purpose of healing sends vibrations in the form of focused positive energy that truly works on the physical plane.

Hormone balancing is a more powerful tool than you can imagine. With no chemical side effects, it assists in your mental and emotional health as well as your physical well-being. It is very handy in relationship difficulties. I find when I am confronting my husband or a friend or family member in speaking my own will, I tend to feel more assertive, more aggressive. That means I am probably pumping more testosterone through my system than usual. This also weighs the situation away from a positive, honoring solution. Being heard is valuable and important, but not if it's at the expense of the one you are speaking to. So when you get into a confrontation where it appears a stalemate is just around the corner, balance your hormones quietly and quickly and you will find the conversation begins to flow more openly and equally. Conversely, if you feel intimidated easily and have great ideas about speaking your word until you are face-to-face with someone, balance those hormones and get yourself in a place of balance, more testosterone probably, and find the courage you so often lose. Remember, this is a tool for you and those you love, not to be used to fix people who haven't asked for fixing. Also, in times of difficulty in a relationship, work on yourself first, assuming that you can alter your reaction to things before you can change someone else to see your viewpoint.

GABRELL'S OPEN HEART

This brings me to the next creative idea for managing relationships. It is what I call *Gabrell's Open Heart*. This is not only
specific to male/female relationship issues, or those that follow
those general male/female roles, but let's begin there since it is the
most stereotypical and easiest to understand. I went to visit a healer
named Gabrell a few years ago who claimed to assist in healing
through the vehicle of the eyes. I wasn't sure how that could be
accomplished, but I was certainly looking for some alternative to
deal with my increasingly poor vision. What I took away from
him was much more than information about how to heal my
physical eyes, even though that was certainly part of it.

He brought my awareness to a pattern that males and females
get involved in every time they get into an emotional discussion.
I don't like to say fight, because it really is about expressing oneself openly, and sometimes heatedly. But fight is really what it
sometimes becomes. The dance goes like this. (Excuse the obvious exaggeration for the purposes of brevity). The male expresses
his opinion full of testosterone and sometimes antagonistically (if
the female plays this part, reverse the roles). The female recoils a
little, combating in words, but going inward all the while to protect herself. Male comes in after her. Keep in mind that in most
cases it is not really the material of the discussion that activates
this dance. It could be about the most insignificant issue. Step
outside your humanness for a moment and see this as a mating
ritual of a most unusual species. As he attacks her even more, she
takes her femaleness and runs away from his male aggression. The
more the attacker jabs, the more she recoils, until she is well inside her heart's castle with the drawbridge pulled up. This infuri-
ates him. Because the whole thing, according to very wise Gabrell,
is about him just wanting to be loved by his woman. Why can't he
just be nice and ask? That's apparently a *chick* thing. Anyway,
now the female is safe inside her protected self, hard shell around

her heart and ready for whatever may come. This is usually when it starts hailing. Good thing, you think, I am safe inside. But, Gabrell says, it would never have rained, much less hailed, if the drama had unfolded differently.

I asked, "Okay, what then?" He says one must maintain an attitude of an open heart no matter what happens in the conversation. My first reaction, and he laughed at my blatant expression of displeasure, was to say, "But it's going to *hurt!*" To which he replied, "You're going to get some *on* you." All right, I said, admittedly reluctant, "Tell me how to do this."

He said that you must first ascertain whether you love your mate, no matter if he believes something you don't, no matter if he challenges everything you believe in or stand for. That was a given in my relationship. All right then, if that's the case, he suggests that when your partner begins to attack your core beliefs, don't run inside. Just stand there, heart wide open and show your gleaming love for him. When he tries to argue, you won't really see the argument anymore. You will see right through the façade and simply love him. You can speak your opinion, but it won't seem personal, because the less you run, the less he chases. Pretty soon, the fire goes out since he got what he subconsciously came for, your open and unconditional love. He was just testing you, "Does she love me? Can I be worthy of being loved no matter how much of an ass I am?" Is it about a mother's unconditional love? I don't know, but I can tell you this. It works.

During my 3 ½ hour drive home from Gabrell's I thought about the open heart the whole way. It made a big impact on me, but I didn't really know if I could do it. For all I preached about love and unconditional love, could I stand there and allow someone to wallop me in my most vulnerable spots? I didn't know if I was that brave. But I owed him and myself the effort to at least try.

Luckily for me, as soon as I got home my practice package was waiting for me. I had been gone two days, my husband was tired of me being gone and, like Gabrell said, wanted to be loved. I don't remember the exact topic, but he started in on me about something that was a core belief, asking attacking questions, shoving my own words at me, something like that. I wanted to recoil and retreat into my studio. But I stood there believing in Gabrell. I forcefully had to hold my heart energy open as I spun the thoughts around in my head, "I love him no matter what he thinks about my beliefs…I love him no matter what he says…I love him" and literally within moments, the storm ended as quickly as it had begun. It was the oddest thing. Gabrell's Open Heart really worked. I just stood there loving him and then amazingly within moments he just fell into my arms. I can't say it isn't hard sometimes, but this isn't for the weak of heart. If you have issues of betrayal or extreme vulnerability in the love department, this may be pretty difficult indeed. Nonetheless, I offer these awarenesses to pick and choose from, depending upon your propensities, willingness and abilities.

Now, about how to actually open the heart. It's one thing to say it, it's another altogether to really *do* it. I will try to describe it the best I can, and you can insert what feelings or emotions are equivalent to them for you. If you can imagine a vortex-like energy doorway residing in front of the heart (as in other areas of the energetic body), it spins open in one direction and closes down in the other in a circular motion, like a whirlpool of sorts, spinning things out as well as in. It responds to our energy. When we are feeling jolly and congenial, it is most likely open and responsive to others. When we are feeling tired and irritated this energy doorway is poised, ready to close or open, depending upon the stimulus. When we feel sad, grief-stricken, or betrayed especially, the door is fairly well closed. These all happen unbeknown to our conscious mind, like involuntary reflexes. Say you wanted to keep a door open when it wanted to shut, you would have to prop it open or stick your foot in there. This is what Gabrell suggests. He says to consciously keep the door open to your significant other (as you get bolder, you can try it with others you trust less). Even or especially when you feel it closing down of its own accord in response to your conditioned patterns, hold the door open. It is hard, trust me.

Imagine a welling up in your chest or heart area, a bigness and fullness, a feeling of genuine love. You are filling that area with energy to keep it from collapsing inward. It feels like it wants to slam with your fingers in it, but once you get the hang of it, it will obey your conscious mind with less effort. The key is being conscious. Your patterning may very well be similar to the male/female dance I discussed earlier, but you must be willing and ready to keep the doorway to your heart open. I can honestly say that no other one single thing has made such a difference in my relationship with my best friend and husband. It has essentially put an end to this male/female game of chase and retreat. New mating rituals can be much more fun! By the way, there is no acceptable ending to this game. He never hears your side, based on what you are sure is logic and you never hear his, what you are equally as certain is based on pure unabated emotion, or vice versa. It is not about winning an argument, it is about something much more subtle and way more important; being loved.

It's the same with kids, I have found, where we engage in the endless loop argument where there is no winner. You don't even feel like you are allowed to ever score one measly point. It isn't about winning, it is about challenging their parent's genuine love. Try the open heart thing with your teenagers. I don't want to underestimate this process with your willful children. I have watched the no-win dynamic played out in parent/child relationships and the *only* thing I have found that can break the stalemate of the nonsensical circular conversation and engagement is this process. What a difference in your home environment it makes. It's like someone has shown you the matrix in which you live, and you see that this verbal argument is a façade and that the core of these emotional interactions is about proving and gaining some

level of real love. You really have to experience it to truly understand the significance of what I am talking about. Gabrell's Open
Heart is only for the strong of heart, or the courageous! By the
way, I only got a *little* on me, and it washes out!

TEN-YEAR-OLD SELF TEST

These ideas are creative ways to enhance relationships, accept
more responsibility for each relationship and break through stag-
nant times. Next I have something that is really fun to do. I was
saving it until after the Open Heart exercise since that was pretty
hard. I am from the school of rewards. If I do something that is
hard for me or have accomplished something that was pretty difficult, I give myself a physical reward. So here is your reward for
trying Gabrell's method. I call it the *Ten-Year-Old Self Test*. This is
how it goes.

Life moves on and unsure of exactly what has transpired, here
you are. It may be a mini van, a few kids, a great dog, new carpeting and an okay job. Some things feel comfortable, but there's
also something that nags about there being more. You are a perfect candidate for the Ten-Year-Old Self Test. Simply imagine
yourself as you were when you were 10, just hanging out and
playing. Remember the grade you were in, your friends, the house
you lived in at the time. See your 10-year-old self in your mind's
eye. Greet yourself and guide your 10-year-old around your present
life. Watch your 10-year-old's reaction. They (the younger version of you) will ultimately point out what they like most and
what they don't. This is the beauty of talking with a 10-year-old.

I loved the movie *The Kid* with Bruce Willis because this exact thing happens. I had been checking in with my own 10-year-
old for years without telling anyone about it, for fear they would
think I was crazy. Then Hollywood showed visually how it could
be done, and in fact, the main character going back to third grade
(or whatever grade it was) with his younger self is really a lot like

the work I do. The movie shows Bruce Willis as an adult and also a young boy to illustrate how we still carry the past with us as long as we have unresolved issues back there. As the two seek to understand what happened when he was a child in a different, less blaming, more mature way, they grow in self-esteem and also joy. Remembering dreams and desires you had when you were 10 helps you as an adult re-find some joyful things you may have lost, but needn't have. Anyway, back to our self-test. In the movie, Bruce Willis' younger self says to him (an affluent, single guy, the envy of every other guy his age), "What? We don't even have a *dog*???" I loved that! Remember, that 10-year-old is *us*! Still. Somewhere in there.

So listen to your own 10-year-old for advice. If he or she is reluctant to say anything, you should be able to read yourself well enough to know what is stymieing him/her. You know how most 10-year-olds are. They are pretty honest and also have an accurate sense of what adults think, well enough to play the game, while part of them still believes in angels and miracles and bogeymen.

So listen. Trash the mini van and get a killer SUV. Or better yet, a truck. Whatever your 10-year-old wants. I got a trampoline when I was almost 40, guess who suggested that? We love it too! I'm not saying that you can or want to indulge your 10-year-old in everything they want, but they will assess your life very honestly and directly. They will either look disappointed, as in *The Kid*, or they will be jumping with glee or somewhere in between. Strangely enough, when you send your energy (that focusing thing again) to yourself at 10 you may find that part of you *is* there. In fact, not to get too esoteric, if time is not linear (Tuesday then Wednesday then Thursday) then maybe it still *is* happening somewhere. That is for another discussion, but suffice it to say, part of you is energetically accessing information from the you of an earlier time.

Let me ask you this. When your mind takes you back down memory lane and remembers something really painful, a time when you were being treated poorly or when you remember someone hurting you very badly, do you ever *feel* that same way again? Like you were reliving it? It is what Carolyn Myss talks about when she says that where we invest our energy becomes our biography or our biology. What she means is, where your energy goes, there you physically go also. You don't like where you are? Move out of there and put your energy somewhere else. Remember, your energy creates your reality, so be careful where you put it. Following this line of thought, accessing yourself as a 10-year-old, random as that may seem, is entirely possible. Quiet your present mind enough to hear and reap their wisdom. See how they respond to your primary partner. Let them check out where you live, what you do for a living, and definitely your pets and your clothes.

I had been living in my present house for about a year when I realized I was living out a childhood dream. I had always wanted a bedroom with those angled, attic type ceilings and for it to be pale purple. Also, ever since I had seen the Walt Disney movie *Thomasina* as a child, I had wanted to be like that compassionate woman who lived in the woods and took care of hurt animals. I never wanted to be a veterinarian, I just wanted to have an innate trust from wild animals, and animals of all kinds. I loved that movie mostly because of the character relegated to live in the woods because the people in the village thought she was unusual. One day I was sitting in my room, looking out the window onto my 100-year-old apricot tree watching the birds which I have been privileged to help and I looked inside my purple, attic-walled room and realized, this is my Thomasina tree and my childhood room and I am becoming that woman. All these things were happening unconsciously. As if the directions had been given a long time ago, but the willingness to follow them had only just come.

Years ago I read a book about the Findhorn Experience, a group of people in the 1960s who took a parcel of fairly infertile land out on the shores of Northern Scotland and created a world-renowned garden, simply by listening to the plants and the devas (or spirits) of the plants, telling them what to put in the soil and how and when to plant. It drew a lot of attention, since their produce was larger and tastier than anything grown in the most fertile of soils. There was an account of this intellectual fellow from London, I believe, who came to become a part of the project and lend what he knew. It tells of an incident when he was in his 60s returning to a spot from his childhood that he had always loved, in the forest, with a pond for wishing. While there he caught a physical glimpse of fairies of the forest, creatures that many believe exist, but few can actually see with the human eye (or mind). He asked why here? Why now? They replied that they remembered him as a child on this very spot wishing more than anything to be able to see these illusive creatures sometime before he died. That childlike belief eventually coupled with an adult concept of reality, but the wish itself never died. He just had to allow himself to believe it was possible, and there they were. As you can imagine, it was a very memorable experience, one at which I'm sure his 10-year-old self was also present and happy as a lark!

Your own children, if you have any, can certainly benefit from this experience too. It may make it easier to see out of their eyes from time to time. If we are closer to our divine essence before we come into this body, then possibly as younger people, we have more intuitive ideas about our soul's desires before we have had a chance to see what society considers successful and shift to different thinking. Take a step back into your purer essence and drink from that wellspring of creative ideas.

MANAGING AN EMOTIONAL WORD LIST

Keeping an emotional word list handy is an idea I share with my clients who are having difficulty developing the self-discipline to control their intensely negative reactions, and to help them understand the source of their emotional buttons. This emotional word list is a list of negative emotions, all the ones you can think of and a few more for good measure. You don't want to use it to dwell on the words, because just their very image can generate a powerfully negative response, as we experience first hand while reading depressing material. Pull it out when you don't know why you are feeling a certain way, but want to get your feelings under control, or at least try your best to deal with them. For example, one of the women I work with said the first time she used it was when she snapped at her husband and then started crying for what seemed like a pretty small incident. She walked away from her husband who was looking rather shocked, as her behavior didn't seem to match his rather insignificant request. She went into her room and took out her emotional word list. She was mad, she thought, she didn't like her husband, she thought, she wanted to run away, but when she read through her two columns of words, the word that jumped out at her (and that's really what it does) was *overburdened*. She felt a sigh of relief and understanding. She wasn't really mad at her husband at all. She wasn't angry. She had just taken on too many things and the sum of them all made the one thing her husband asked her to do feel like 14 tons. It was the straw that broke the camel's back. Once she became aware that she was overburdened, she could deal with that. She could reallocate some of the things she had to do and/or set aside some things she wanted to do until later. She could prioritize and lighten her load, truly within minutes. And she did. She returned downstairs, feeling lighter and composed and smiled at her husband. I'm sure her husband thought it was just one of the mysteries of being a woman.

So it works very simply. You can either put together your own word list, or you can photocopy the one I have compiled at the end of the book. They are the most common emotions I find in my clients and myself. You may want to omit some or add others. When you feel confused emotionally, and don't understand why you are reacting to someone or something as you are, when someone pushes your buttons without any trouble, when you are plagued by emotions for which you can't find the source, when you feel unsettled, but you don't understand why, pull out your list. Relax, try not to have any preconceived ideas about what you are feeling. Just be as neutral as possible. Then slowly read silently through the list. Go from back to front, down to up, side to side, varying the way you read it, and allow the vibration to find its fit. That's just what it is. Emotions are vibrations. Each one very specific, and if there is no common resonance, you will pass the word by without a flicker. As soon as you see or read the emotion that is currently taking up residence in your energy system, you will actually *feel* it. And feel means something different to everyone. Some people feel or confirm something with a nice set of goose bumps or bristly hairs behind their neck. Others get moist eyes, still others feel a particular knowing in their gut. Whatever it is for you, get friendly with this physical indicator and rely on its wisdom. It will come in handy more often than not.

You may need to read the list more than once if you feel the emotion is there, but you can't zero in on it. Relax, shut your eyes and try again. If you have read the list and nothing is resonating, it may not be there. In that case, you will have to be creative. If you are good at getting messages from your inner wisdom, ask to see or know or feel the word. If not, you may ask what is the *closest* word that is on the list. I find that is very helpful, then you can either get a fairly good message from the similar word, or the exact word then pops up from the similar word.

What to do once you have discovered the word? Well, it depends on you and what the word is and what you want to do about it. What if it is anger? Figure out what you're feeling angry about. Ask yourself, "What or who is making me angry?" Then go through all the present situations you are in. Is it my mother, my boss, the barking dog next door? Is it that I am angry that I am being asked to do something I really don't want to do and am mad at myself for being so wimpy? When the situation that you are feeling angry about surfaces in your conscious mind, you will have a physically emotional reaction. You may feel a little reaction with each suggestion since you are already feeling angry. Everything in your world is adding fuel to your anger. You will also be attracting more of the vibration of anger, as like energies attract more of the same, but when you get to the main issue underlying the anger, you will know it. There will be no doubt.

Getting to the source of the anger may be a problem, because you may not want to see it, consciously or not, and so you have to sit and look at every aspect of your present life and pull in things that appear farfetched, that may indeed be the culprit. Then what? You figure it out. Maybe it's something such as, "I am being expected to do such and such and I really don't want to, but cannot find the strength to say otherwise." Therein lies your teacher. You have been presented with an obstacle that you will grow by overcoming, but it is not a given that you can or will. At least you will know what is going on, instead of just sitting around fuming and kicking the cat. Now it is your decision to act upon your emotional indicators or to suppress them or to turn them loose on someone much less intimidating. I am only here to try to hand you some tools with which you can travel and survive along the journey, and hopefully make the best of the trip!

Another possibility is that after using your emotional word list for a year or so, you start to find that at the core of a *lot* of your emotionally charged situations is the same word or similar words, such as worthless or unwanted, for example. Take heed, there is a subtle vibration that is haunting your energy system and coloring your world. That may be the call to seek additional assistance to help uncover the deeper source of these sabotaging resonances in your world. After all, everyone who deals in energy, all living beings, will be responding to your energetic self, not the one that you try to convince them you are.

Again, I am reiterating my main theme which is, *you cannot change others, you can only strive to change yourself and your reaction to them.* What I often find is that people who are stuck in a particular unpleasant emotion, like self-hate or powerlessness, tend to see the whole world colored through those lenses. Pretty soon, they begin to think they are evil or bad people, always in a foul mood, looking at the worst side of everything. This increases the negativity with which they are already resonating. It is a circle game, taking all self-esteem down with it in its spiral. Feeling powerless creates feelings of aimlessness, which allow feelings of aloneness or separateness, which harbors feelings of being un-wanted and then self-pity, and pretty soon increased feelings of being inferior and so on. The recognition of the particular emo-tion and its source, if it can be found, greatly aids in stopping this downward spiral and getting its momentum redirected in a more positive direction.

Once you uncover that you are only feeling powerless because there is one person in your life you have given power to by mis-takenly identifying that person as your ultimate authority figure, then you can reclaim your own energy/power/authority and within a relatively short period of time, recapture your self-esteem. I hear clients complain all the time, "But it's the president of the univer-sity telling me I have to do it, what choice do I have?" My re-sponse is the same as if it were your innocuous neighbor. If it does not honor you, and you have no desire to do it, and you are not being compensated fairly, you have every right and, in fact, obli-gation to yourself, to say no. Sometimes it is the very job you are trying to protect, by submitting to undesirable agreements, that is killing you slowly. Stopping the unwilling submission creates a set of events that, even though possibly producing insecurity at the time, leads to a much more enjoyable and therefore profitable career or job eventually. The line may not be direct, but we have followed the path of evolution through the whole book, finding challenges and teachers at every turn. Remember, if your heart isn't in what you are doing, the Divine isn't in it and the fluidity and synchronicity that create bountiful results aren't there either. So doing what you love will net you greater rewards, not just emotionally and spiritually, but financially as well. So as you are analyzing these emotional vibrations, ask yourself, do I need to expand my set of possibilities to solve this?

One of the activities we do in my creativity workshops is to imagine what we would like to be, given no limitations, and we share those. The task is to believe that you still *can* be that person or at least do something that relates to the dream profession, to work towards it, understanding that the limitations we perceive are only in us! I ask for volunteers to share their dream selves and at one workshop, the first guy to speak up was a math professor about to retire. He had spent his whole life in academia and thoroughly thought of himself as a math professor (he even *looked* like a math professor). So when he confessed that he wanted to be a singer more than anything, we were all a bit taken aback. He immediately gave us his barriers. "I'm too old. I live in a small town with no voice teachers of any caliber. No one would support me in this venture or want to hear me." My job as facilitator was to expand their world of possibilities, to let them know that the limitations they possessed were just an illusion. I told him that it had just come to my awareness that very week that a world-renowned soprano had just moved to our little town and was teaching. The support that rumbled from the rest of the students showed him that all of us would *love* to hear his suppressed creativity come to fruition in song! His limitations were slowly fading, and with each moment he was getting closer to his dream. In his case, to solve his problem, or quest, he had to get outside the limiting patterns of his overdeveloped brain.

So, you have your emotional word list, you have the inspiration to use it, now you just have to be your own best friend to put it into the action required to elicit change. If you feel enthusiastic or compelled, look at the positive word list and plant a few of those in place of the negative ones you removed.

SPEAKING TO THE HIGHER SELF

This next tool is a handy, easy, yet very powerful way to create an atmosphere of honor and harmony in any relationship. It is actually talking to someone's *higher self*. When you have tried to talk to someone where understanding and communication were vital, but nothing shifted, often you have reached a stalemate with their ego or exterior personality. Whether or not they are stubborn, unyielding or just prideful, many things can cause a person to want to stand their ground spitefully. We've all been there. This technique is about bypassing the ego and talking directly to the humble, willing and harmony-seeking part of them. You do not need to be in the presence of this person, in fact, it is easier if you are not, because the emotions they inflame in you can be subdued. You simply picture your person, whoever they are, and say, "*I want to speak with the higher self of —person's name —.*" You can do this aloud or silently. You directly tell them everything you need to say. That's all. You cannot lie. A higher self knows when you are not telling the truth. You are dealing with the kindest, most soulful part of this person, so being kind is necessary. They get the message. You may have to talk to them several times, because if their ego is stuck in a very negative state, they may not be able to hear their own inner guidance. So if you try a few different times, hopefully one time will get through.

The results are astounding. I mentioned this concept to a woman having a very difficult divorce. She had been married 20 years and had been miserable, so being divorced was a welcome relief. However, her ex-husband was giving her so much grief, using their teenage son as a weapon, that she was seriously distraught. All attempts to communicate sincerely and honestly failed. She tried to remind him that he also had been miserable and she wished he could find someone more compatible and have a truly happier life. He was stuck on making her pay for leaving him. He fought her about decisions that involved their son and refused to help support her decisions when the son was with him. It was a veritable stalemate. With this suggestion, she left my office and went home that night and spoke to his higher self. She thought it was a bit weird, but was willing to try anything. She said that she visualized her ex-husband and told him what was really on her heart. She got it all out. Not in a nasty way, but in an honest, open way. In her mind's eye, he begged and pleaded with her to not cut the chord they had, however negative. She imagined a dark chord holding them together and cut it. He began fading. Then her son's face appeared. He began pleading on behalf of his father. She spoke to his higher self also. She said she would always have a loving relationship with him, but not *through* his father. She cut the negative chord there too and watched him fade, unsure of what was happening. Then she went to bed. The next day, her ex-husband called and said they had been fighting too long and he wanted to be friends and would support her in whatever decisions she made that involved their son, and he was ready to let her go and move on with his life. The *very next* day! Needless to say, after two years of stalemate and bickering, she almost fell over dead. She has since taken this technique to the boardroom of her company, to create harmony and cooperation in business dealings and create a more fulfilling work environment as well, with equally astonishing results.

The telling of this story also provides a perfect example to reiterate the primary thesis of this entire book. This woman had remarried when she cut the ties with her ex-husband. Her new husband had a very similar story, with similar experiences with his ex-wife. Even after seeing the miraculous results of his wife's *tie-cutting* experience, he has remained consciously unwilling to do the same with the higher self of his ex-wife. He has made the decision to carry the hate with him. That is part of his journey and should be honored. If, or when, or where, or how he ever chooses to leave that hate behind, is his decision alone. We all walk our path at our own speed.

Once I was speaking to the higher self of a young boy I was working with. I was trying to get him to open up to the possibility of love. I told him that his mother loved him. Immediately, I heard him say to me, "No, she does not" and knew it was true. I rephrased the comment to say, she loves you to the extent to which she is presently able to love. He understood that and accepted it. Speaking to someone's higher self is not about manipulation, that isn't possible. You are dealing with the wisest part of them, they will not simply listen to you and obey your every command. It doesn't work like that. They will, however, respond to honesty and truth, unlike their egoic counterpart oftentimes.

Instead of banging your head against a brick wall, go around the brick wall and enter peacefully through the garden. Find the most pleasant part of someone and greet them there. This also challenges us to be in a space of integrity, because we cannot get away with just whining and begging for what we desire, but we must present a case that is heartfelt and in the best interest of *both* parties. In the case of the divorced couple, the ex-wife helping the ex-husband understand that it was truly over and that it was in the best interest of all three of them was genuinely positive for all parties concerned.

Let me give you another example. Say you have a mother-in-law who is very egotistical and prideful. She refuses help from anyone and when you try to give her something, always finds a way to give it back. You care for her, but know that she will not allow herself to receive whatever you or anyone offers in the form of help or support. She is now getting on in age and genuinely needs assistance, but her stubborn, prideful self is still refusing. Stop trying to connect with her egoic self. There is a seriously intense wall there, created over a lifetime. Bypass that and speak to her higher self, regularly. Tell her that if she needs anything materially or spiritually, you are there for her. You can let her know that you support her even though her brain does not know it. Let her know that as her time draws near, to leave this realm, you will assist her. You are lending spiritual support that is invaluable. It will even provide a sense that she is not as alone as she likes to tell her egoic self. This type of connection offers greater rewards than trying to shove yourself into her life in ways that she will reject, leaving you both feeling resentful.

What if the person you really need to talk to has already passed on? You can still talk to them. They continue to exist and can hear you. It will have the most peaceful results, helping the deceased let go of negative chords as well as helping you.

Don't forget to talk to children and animals. You can even connect with those in your life who are not so coherent, those who have Alzheimer's or cerebral palsy or are in the final stages of cancer or are mentally missing altogether. I once tried this with my neighbor's lovely little shitzu puppy. He was peeing in the house and after several months of their trying to potty train him, he was definitely walking on thin ice. They were a retired couple, the greatest family for this young dog, but he was about to be returned to the previous owner. I had grown pretty attached to this little pup myself, so after the wife confided to me that he had one more day, and if he made a mess, they couldn't do it anymore and would return him, I tried speaking to his higher self. I told him that these people loved him dearly and would spoil him and give him the best life if only he would stop peeing inside. I explained what he was to do, how he could go to the door and bark, be let out and all would be well. I let him know that he was greatly loved. The next day, my neighbor was amazed when he had suddenly taken to barking at the door and henceforth has not made any indoor accidents. Talking to pets before moving, neutering, or giving them away truly helps the transition.

Talking to the higher selves of children who are too young to understand spoken words is almost too easy. Remember, asking to speak to their higher self, being honest and communicating for the benefit of both parties is the key. I have tried this, I must admit, in situations where the outcome would be only one-sided,

what I want. For example, communication such as this to desperately want a dog to stop barking at night has very little effect.
Obviously, the dog needs something that barking will secure, or
so she thinks. So, to reiterate, to promote understanding, to bring
harmony and help another comprehend your viewpoint, speaking with another's higher self is the answer.

You have to be ready to be heard or to forgive or to let go,
whatever the results will accord. You cannot cut a chord of negativity and still hold on to *any* negative emotions to that person.
When the timing is right, you will be ready just as the husband of
the woman who cut the ties to her ex-husband will find. Then
you dig this tool out from this book.

As you have seen in many anecdotes in this book, communicating and developing a relationship with Nature has proven to
be positive on many occasions. When speaking to your animals,
don't limit yourself. You also have access to your plants and even
rocks and the sculpturing of your gardens by connecting to the
highest energy of all things. I believe we have much to learn and
can gain unique wisdom from connecting to the rest of Nature.
When planting bulbs in my flower gardens, I often ask them where
they would like to be located, since I am not sure what color they
will be and how they interact with other flowers and plants around
them. Invariably, the results are far more stunning than if I had
planned them with my brain. I do the same with houseplants. I
may have a place in mind for a particular plant because of aesthet-
ics, but the plant always tells me if that is not where it wants to
be. I obey the plant, because I know it will thrive if it is where it
would prefer to be. Trust me, I've tried both ways.

Normally, I suggest speaking to the higher self of the entity in
question in the privacy of your mind. Many people will be un-
nerved if they hear you talking to the shrubbery, and the spoken
voice isn't necessary anyway. Once while planting some young
flowers along the side of my house I was speaking to them and
carrying on a whole conversation as they directed me to their

growing spots. I was sure I was doing this in my head, but after awhile, my husband stepped out and asked me where the children went. I said, "What children?" He said, "The ones you were just talking to for so long. I heard you. It was so precious." I was positive it had all been conducted in the labyrinth of my mind, but I guess some got out!

Along this same line is the concept of sending thoughts to another. If thoughts are just energy in invisible form, they still do hold power. Therefore, if you always think negative thoughts about someone, they will receive your thoughts as energy and this only worsens whatever reason you have to think poorly of them in the first place. If you have someone in your life that you care about, but they are in a very negative and angry space, every time you think of them and think negative thoughts such as, "Oh, that poor slob, what a sorry loser," you are, in fact, sending that vibration to resolidify his or her own lack of self-worth. Instead, connect with their higher self when you think of them and send positive loving thoughts. That's often all you can do for this person. I get asked quite often what my client can do for their son or daughter who they feel is on a spiraling downward and destructive path. Many times they are not in communication and feel cut off from any visible means of supporting or assisting this person. They want me to wave a wand and bring their prodigal son home. I don't do that, even if I could, it would not honor their own journey. As I mentioned before, being in a dark cave is sometimes where our soul needs to journey for growth or understanding. What I do offer is this concept of thoughts as energy. Send positive thoughts of encouragement and support and acceptance, if they are genuine. If you cannot go that far, at least let them know you are concerned and care about them. They will receive this energy message and even though you may not get their immediate feedback, it may be the ray of hope that keeps them from total darkness.

I mentioned earlier about intelligent dark energies as forces in the physical universe and here again, when we send negative thoughts to anything, whether it is a person, a war, a policy or a country, we are simply feeding the dark intelligences. Instead of opposing it, as we think we are, we are enhancing the negative behavior. In 2003, when our country was going to war with Iraq there was opposition all over the globe. People were screaming out against Bush and the administration and being cynical and using foul language and generally engaging in opposition through obvious methods of disapproval. Not that it did any good, but a few days before the threatened bombing actually began in Baghdad, a different voice was heard. There was a group of children in Hawaii, called the Psychic Children, that sent out an appeal to project messages of love and light to Bush and the leaders of Iraq instead of fueling the fire with more negativity and hate. There was a call to join together on a certain date to offer this energetic vigil for peace. The idea was exactly in keeping with the elements of dark forces, do not fuel the fire; squelch it with light and love. Our country still went to war and Baghdad was bombed and many lost their lives, but somewhere a seed was planted, fighting war with war, even if it is for no war, has not worked and never will by the very energetic nature of the Universe, but offering the vibration of light and love is the only hope.

So be creative, offer whatever tools you have to your relationships. Don't allow yourself to feel trapped in a corner with no solutions. There are always solutions, you just have to expand your possibilities and open the gates on your own limiting boundaries.

10 The Spiritual Self

HAVING A RELATIONSHIP WITH YOURSELF

The most difficult, but definitely most profound concept I am going to offer is the ability or willingness to have a loving relationship with yourself. This truly seems to be where all divine relationships begin. When I was younger I used to hear that you must be able to love yourself before you can love another. At the time, I thought that was nonsense. I loved people and they loved me back, but I didn't genuinely love myself. What I found through time and experience was the quality of that love, filled with conditions and limitations, related directly to the quality of the relationship, so I would reword that old adage to be, "You have to divinely love yourself to have a divine relationship with someone else."

As we have already discovered, there are many ways to have a relationship with the self, from adversarial to worshipping and everything in between. From years of energy healing sessions, what has become glaringly apparent to me is that somehow many people have attached to their highest, most divine self a sense of unworthiness. The blooming of this highest self is the one I suggest we encourage. Perhaps you haven't really looked at what kind of relationship you have with yourself. You simply function, survive, do the best you can, heal what you can, avoid what you can and make do the rest of the time.

What if you wanted to open lines of communication or get to know this highest self, or our Divine Essence? I would first suggest you examine the guts of your internal dialogue. This is the telltale sign of relations with the self. If you speak to yourself out loud or in your mind in a negative way, ever, let's look at that. I know one fellow who mumbles to himself while he works about what a loser he is and how he could never do anything right the first time. He even uses names for himself that sound a lot like what his father might have called him. His father is dead, but the voice remains. He has continued the relationship in his head until it has now become his own. Needless to say, he doesn't think a lot of himself. As an aside though, he does a perfectionist's job in whatever he does. How we see ourselves, by the way, is usually very different from how others view us.

Do you encourage yourself, hearing things like, "You can do it, go ahead and cross that bridge, or go ahead and face that fear, I'm right here with you?" Do you sabotage yourself with internal comments like, "Go ahead, try that new thing, but you will fail, I've seen it before, happens every time, what's so different now?" Do you believe in yourself? Do you try new things and encourage yourself and celebrate when you succeed, even if not to perfect standards? Do you dislike yourself? Would you marry or date someone like you? Would you trust someone like you? Do you feel you are a fake, everything you are respected for somehow feels like a lie? Do you feel that no matter what you do, if only people could see inside your head, they would be shocked because it is not what you present? Do you hate yourself, truly hoping that you will get run over by a Mack truck? Do you hide things that you feel are dark from those you want to love you, thinking they would no longer love you or even be afraid if they had a glimpse of those dark parts of you? Do you try to hide those things from yourself? Do you ignore your inner voices? Are they too mean, or too kind?

As you can see, there are as many ways to have a relationship with the self as there are to find the way back to the Divine, one for every human who exists! What I want you to do is try to analyze how you exist with yourself. Are you sympathetic and positive on the outside, but somewhere subconsciously are not allowing yourself to live the life you feel you have every right to? Or are you unintentionally sabotaging the wonderful things that are trying to come your way? These are what I call human programs we carry within us, which limit our ability to truly have a divine relationship with ourselves that could then lead to the potential of having a divine relationship with others. The process of removing or changing these programs can be a first step in having a more positive, nurturing relationship with oneself.

HUMAN PROGRAMMING

My premise, as I have mentioned earlier in the book, is that we are all created from the fabric of divinity. The seed or core of us is Divine, not evil, dark or corrupted. There are many things and many centuries worth of negativity heaped upon that divine seed however. Hence, the knowledge that we are even light beings at all has also been occluded. Those things we pile upon our own individual selves may require lifetimes or years or just subtle awarenesses to remove, but they are our own. I have presented many ideas about how relationships show up in our lives at just the right time to challenge these old negative images or beliefs about ourselves or life in general. What I want to look at now is more of what would come under the category of consensus reality. That is a mass illusion that we all support. We don't know what is outside of our mass illusion, or consensus reality, because no one supports any other possibility. We all find boundaries in our own lives and go beyond them, but has anyone gone beyond the illusion that physical walls are not penetrable by a physical being? Richard Bach in his book entitled *Illusions: The Adventures of a Reluctant Messiah* gives us a glimpse into another potential reality where the ground is like water and water behaves like the earth. Who is to say what actually are properties of earth since the earth behaves in all sorts of ways, from unmovable granite to flowing magma? We all belong to a group of illusions. I want to look at the consensus reality that we have bought into that limits our highest self, that prevents us from being all we came here to be, and that creates a barrier between having divine relationships or just settling for mediocrity. This is what I call human programming.

Let me give you some examples and show you how to activate this process. You begin with the query, "What human programming limits me from knowing I am completely Divine?" If you can honestly answer, "Nothing," you are either finished with this book or you are hearing an answer to another question. Some of the responses I have heard from my clients are "humans and their makers are separate," or "humans are not worthy," or "the human incarnation is painful and sorrowful, not supposed to be joyful." These are things we have learned through consensus reality, as a human group, from our elders from their elders, through our media, from our language (life sucks, then you die), and from our own interpretation of the experiences of human life. They also may not necessarily be true.

This is the lovely part. If they are programs—and you have to go along with that assumption with me—they can be reprogrammed. If we are born believing that the trees are multiple shades of blue, not green, we soon find out we are wrong and everyone else is right. Why? Because everyone can't be wrong. There really isn't a place for you to see something that differently. It challenges the consensus reality we all live in. That is what makes it consensus; we all believe and support it.

Fitting in and belonging has always been an attribute developed for the longevity of individuals, for the purpose of survival. We need the group support of tribes (and I don't just mean indigenous people, I mean anything that ties a group of people together through a common bond) and the safety it brings with it. As we move through our evolving soul experience, the inevitable process of growth involves individuation. That means separating from our tribe, or established ties to a society or religion that support a certain set of unquestionable beliefs. As painful as it invariably becomes, separating from those unmovable beliefs is a prerequisite for the soul's evolution. One must begin to question the boundaries of their beliefs to find the limits or lack of them in their life. How does one find their highest self while firmly situated in a six foot square box? Growth of the soul is no different than that of a seed. The seed's natural propensity is to grow towards the light. The soul is no different. My hope is that by removing some of the rocks sitting atop your divine seed, the path to reach the light won't be as cumbersome and distorted. It will be clear and strong.

Can we seek our highest selves individually and still support each other, finding our unique and purposeful traits and gifts without challenging consensus reality? Shouldn't we challenge consensus reality? Isn't the Earth herself also evolving? So what happens when you support a consensus reality that applies to the past, but not to the new spiritual you of the present? How do you reprogram your subconscious self? Maybe you just need to update your programming software. How do you even find out what programs you are running?

Begin by asking yourself this question, and sorry to say, no one can help you do this, not even your guides or nonphysical helpers. This is very clear to me, it must come out by the one who accepted it: you! Ask, "What human programming limits me from knowing I am wholly and completely Divine?" Allow yourself to be in a quiet place, where you can hear the answers. Try not to have any preconceived ideas, remember, we are all divinely unique. I put my clients on a scale of 0-10, ten being the most occluded with negative programming that is presently accessible and zero being completely clear or nothing available for reprogramming. (If you feel unable to sense where you are on the scale, just continue to ask until there are no more answers, realizing that the closer you get to zero, or all you can access right now, the more difficult the answers may be to find). I continue to encourage my clients to search for their answers until they register zero. Each limiting program that is removed takes you closer to zero. Do not stop before you reach zero, why would you want to? The way to access these answers is to realize that your brain does not hold the answers. It may come up with all of the latest, most popular ways to limit oneself, and what may feel trendy or logical, but this is probably not it. You need to ask the above question and then let your awareness fall into your heart area. Let your heart hear the question and let your heart answer. You will know when you have unearthed the old program and not its fake. A feeling on your part, to confirm its truth, will corroborate it.

For example, you find the answer "To be a human is to be in exile from my true nature," now what do you do? You reprogram that. It is similar to running an out-of-date program on your computer. Too many of the newer programs you are running will not be compatible with the old one, so you are finally forced to pull out your wallet and pop for the updated version. We are doing the same thing, and it is usually prompted by exactly the same reason, there are too many new programs that are not compatible with this antiquated way of thinking/feeling/knowing. You state something like this in your own words, "I choose to remove this limiting human programming and replace it with the knowledge that being a human is only one small aspect of my true nature and that the Divine would not have created this existence without this human nature being yet another possible way of expressing my Divine Nature. I do not believe I am in exile from my Divine Self or the Divine Creator, I am living in my highest self with my support coming from divinity." You may need to speak more mental words, you may need to simply envision something, you may need to be more convincing, but it is uniquely your way that will allow this programming to be removed. Sometimes my clients describe an image that comes to them that fills them with knowing, or a sense of something that they didn't know before. You have the code, you put the programming in, so allow yourself to be open to finding the key to decode this non-truth and use it.

Let's say you are having trouble getting more than two programs. Allow the space to be silent and go deeper, do not allow the distractions that will introduce themselves to be entertained. Sit and wait, keep asking the question, what is keeping me from knowing I am Divine? Eventually, the response will come. What if you find an answer like "human life is based on hate?" What if your conscious mind believes that as well? Being a good salesman or convincing yourself with your brain will not be the answer. You must allow your higher energy self to locate and bring to your mind the key or the password to unlocking this old programming. Whatever you need to say, understand or feel, you will be guided to go there. One woman I worked with was bombarded with a thousand voices all saying she didn't know the answer, what was expected from her, how could she possibly figure it out, why had I never asked anything like this of her before, it was over, she couldn't get it and so on until after ten minutes of silence she finally allowed the awareness of the question to sink into her chest area. As soon as it did, her mental chatter stopped and she instantly was shown a picture that was exactly the greatest obstacle to her highest self-esteem. Another woman I worked with didn't really understand with her brain what I was asking her to do. The reprogramming worked incredibly well though, as if by bypassing her brain circuitry we were able to access the energy system directly. One of the images she received while working towards zero on my scale was of a warm light pouring over her, coming out of her own head. It shocked her to see such a thing, so clear and vivid, knowing it was meant for her when she didn't really comprehend with her brain what the question even was. The result was the same, unlocking the old programming, allowing for a more expansive awareness of life's possibilities.

One thing to keep in mind as you are eliminating human programs is that all around you, in many parts of your reality, many of the things that support the same old programming are still continuing. You have to consciously choose to ignore them or stay firm in your new programming. This is key. All life won't instantly become a flowering rose garden after this moment, although it will feel a lot lighter and more beautiful. In Yehuda Berg's interesting book, *72 Names of God*, he looks at a rabbinical study of the Hebrew characters cryptically chosen in a certain order from the Torah to empower others with the images and power of Divine Nature for healing. He makes a profound observation at the beginning of the book. He says that essentially three things are necessary before the power of these Hebrew characters can be imparted to the reader; 1) a belief that this practice is possible, 2) a belief that you can do it, and 3) the concrete realization that you must take affirmative action when confronted with this past negative behavior. Number three is paramount. Know ahead of time you will be bombarded with human programming, you must be the action verb. Action verbs do not modify, describe or quantify, they act. Be diligent about resisting and conscious of infinite human programming directed your way, however subtle. Eventually, your new programming will have overridden the old so firmly that you will not be nearly as open to this particular consensus reality. Just be aware of other ways you could be influenced.

Here's another program, fairly common in its variations. "While in the human form, I cannot embody the highest vibration of divinity, there are simply limitations of matter." Do we still contain the knowledge that we would not exist in this form if we were not capable of being another expression of the Creation Energy or Divine Nature? That, in fact, the Divine lives in us and our deepest calling and longings are prompted by the Divine wanting to be expressed in exactly the way we most desire. To deny that longing is to deny the Divine its unique expression that only you can fulfill and also deny yourself the greatest life you could imagine! What about ones like "I'm not special, or I am unworthy, or not good enough to house the Divine"? That is actually true nonsense. A Truth of the Universe says (don't take my word for it, feel it in your soul), "You are a divine radiant light being, created from love, for love, and unique, unlike any other." That sounds pretty special, we're all special.

Some programming may actually have been a truth for humans at one time in our history, but is no longer applicable. For example, "My will to survive and protect myself will override every spiritual desire." That may have been true as a lower-developed spiritual being, but now we are moving through multidimensionality and the soul is becoming more in charge so that is no longer a truth.

I mentioned earlier about this scale of 0-10. In listening to your responses and releasing them, ask then, where am I now on this scale of limitations? You may hear a seven or a six or four, but the idea is that you want to get closer to zero and eventually all the way to zero. The last ones tend to be the hardest to uncover, but don't give up. Sometimes you get a response that actually is another way of wording one you've already done. Ask if this will take you closer to your Divine Self. Sometimes it feels that it has been done or we need to reword it in a more inclusive way. You don't want to leave anything out that is part of this human programming. When you are finished, my experience is that you will feel clearer, lighter and have an overall calmer sense of yourself. One woman told me after removing these blocks, she felt happier than she had felt in a very long time and felt a great deal of love for her mother, sister and brother, whom she had not spoken with in years. What we are doing is getting things out of the way that keep us from our most Divine Selves, which is the most loving part of us, so don't be surprised if it opens you up as a vessel of love. You may even find yourself as a light magnet, glowing and attracting people because of the light and love you generate. Talk about being ready to love others!

I don't want to underestimate the profundity of this exercise. If you are only halfhearted when you do it, that is what you will get out of it, but if you wholly experience this and allow your inner heart to speak and release, it truly can change your life forever. Many of my clients have responded to me later that they had no idea at the time how meaningful removing this human programming would be, but it has become a doorway to something much bigger and more awesome. When you change the core way you see yourself, moving from negative to more positive, you have essentially given yourself a new set of lenses by which you view everything in your world.

SPEAKING WITH OUR GUIDES FOR GREATER WISDOM

The universe is pretty orderly and has some pretty understandable laws. One is that while in the human incarnation, learning what we came here to learn, fulfilling our obligations, we can have all the assistance we want and need, but we must ask for it. I imagine that there are all of these beings, of many forms and designs, doing their own specific tasks all hanging around us, dying to hear us utter the words, "Will you help me?" They sit there for years, patiently knowing someday their moment will come, because they are challenged and grow through the assistance they give us. We are all so very interconnected. We are not just the dumb ones needing help, they are given their own growth potential depending on how and what they can do to assist those in this realm. They respect our free will. We are the creatures on Earth that have free will. (Incidentally, the dark energies in our lives do not respect our free will. Keep that in mind. That means they have no problem using or accessing our information against us, without our express permission, as unscrupulous teachers).

A tomato seed when planted and watered will grow to be a tomato, not a palm or a daffodil. There are variations on a theme and each plant has individual features, but they all share in the same frequency or vibration of being a tomato.

Humans on the other hand can do anything they want, literally. Even though a human seed grows to become a human, there are extreme variations based on individual will as opposed to physical variations. Each human has their own unique vibration which comes from the beliefs, the illusions, the decisions, and the choices of the particular individual. Free will is a huge part of our incredible learning experience here on Earth. So, our helpers, no matter how much they have the capability to help, cannot do so until we first ask. Then, watch out! But not until then. They are not being cruel, watching and not assisting in times of huge crisis and pain in our lives, they trust that everything is unfolding just as it should, and they know that we will all find what we seek eventually.

Now that you've decided to ask, what do you ask? How do you ask? What is the difference between talking to yourself and talking to your guides? How do you distinguish the voices or the feelings that follow the asking? A most frequently asked question is, "Once I have asked, how do I hear? Is it my voice I hear or is it theirs? How do I tell the difference?"

I worked with a man in his 70s who had been a minister for many years. After our session together, he asked me who I was talking to when I was asking questions about him. He said, "You were so accurate in your knowledge of my young childhood about things I never told you, yet you knew. How?" I told him I was talking at that particular time to his guardian angel, that when I can't access something we need to know about someone's past, the one being that I know is always there with them is their guardian angel. They tell me. Sometimes I get the answer in a voice, sometimes in a full scene like a movie unfolding, and sometimes just a knowing. He was stunned. I asked, "Why are you so shocked? You are a minister, don't you believe in angels?" He answered that he had studied in the scriptures about angels and said he believed in them, but it was all in theory. I asked what he talked to his parishioners about when they were looking for comfort in times of deep despair. He said, once again, all this knowledge came from theory. He came back several days later and said he had something to ask me. I said okay. "How do I get in touch with my angels?" he wanted to know. I said you just start talking to them and wait for an answer. "Just like that?" Just like that.

Several weeks went by and I didn't hear from the minister trying to form a relationship with angels at 70 years old. Then he came by again asking if he could run something past me. I said sure. He said he felt like he was getting the guidance he had been asking for, but wasn't sure and doubted it. I asked what the guidance was telling him and if he was unhappy with the message. He said he was being told he should reroute his ministry into the prisons and do prison ministry. Coincidentally, since he had begun asking for this career guidance, every fluid thing began happening to lead him into a position where he not only would be ministering to inmates, but would have a hand in restructuring the prisons in our state. I asked, "Is this something you don't want to do?" He replied that indeed he had dreamt of doing this for many years, but never could take the step and if he had his druthers, this would be exactly what he would love to do. I still didn't see the problem. He just needed me to confirm that indeed his guidance will take him where his heart desires, not his least desirable place on the planet. That's the amazing thing about getting assistance that is wise. He left a very happy man!

There is one thing I need to clarify, and that is that most people have this puritan work ethic carryover from our forefathers that makes them believe that if they were really doing what they were called to do in service for the Big Guy, that it would be unpleasant, if not difficult or even painful. That it would mean sacrifice and boredom and elevator music. My understanding is that in your heart is love and what you would love to do is dictated by the feelings of the heart. If it is true that God is love, or the energy of the Universe is unconditional love, then wouldn't this Divine Being express its nature through our hearts? And if we came here to express the Divine through our unique self, how would the Divine be able to do that? Though our hearts. I suggest looking at ourselves (humans, uniquely) as a combination of three parts: our personality (physical self), our soul (spiritual self) and our karma (our set of unique beliefs and experiences). We are just that, three parts, waiting for an assignment. What should we do with this completely unique and irreproducible personage we have here that we call me? We send electricity to it. It enlivens it. That electricity is the very life-force energy of the Universe, or the wellspring of creativity. So plug that power into yourself and what comes out the other side? A product, or representation of creativity that only you could produce. In fact, that may be what we are doing here, expressing the Divine Energy of the Universe in the way only we uniquely can. Maybe that is what we were created for, to be another facet of the incredible multidimensionality of the face of God. So, what I am saying is, if we do not do what we love to do or long to do, we are holding back the expression of the Divine. We are keeping ourselves from being a vehicle of creative energy.

Suffice it to say that what we most want in our heart of hearts is where our guides will guide us in decisions and choices, even if we aren't consciously aware of what is in our heart of hearts. Remember, the voice of the loins can sound a lot like the heart speaking, but it is coming from a different source, not necessarily to be ignored, just not the voice I am referring to.

That being said, you don't have to be afraid that your guides, assuming you ask, and assuming you listen, and assuming you heed their advice, will ever direct you to some dreaded place, doing something you can't stand. That doesn't mean they won't direct you into confronting fears, that is different. Fears are those things that hold power over us when we could be expending our energy in other, more valuable places.

Back to guides, this is very important. When you begin to ask for assistance, you must clean out a pathway. When you get out a dusty old instrument from the attic, it needs to have the cobwebs cleaned out of it and some music forced through it before it will sound beautiful again. It is similar to that when beginning to communicate with nonphysical beings of another realm. First of all, what station do they broadcast on anyway? There is a relatively easy answer, but it is harder still to do. The frequency they operate on is the same one as the feeling of love. If you begin your conversation with, "I am so stupid and bad that anything I do turns out terrible, could you help me?" then you are already setting the frequency up to be one of 'dislike of self' and that is not the frequency on which this communication can best take place. Instead, try tuning in by saying, "I know that being a human has difficult trials and I am in one, but I know I have a beautiful soul under here somewhere and want to become closer to that Divine Self, and farther from this place I am in now. What do you suggest?" Don't ask for an answer that would limit you, such as which should I do, A or B? That limits their choices in responding. They may have a great suggestion that is neither A nor B. They usually do.

We have the initiative and the willingness, now we just need to get in the right frame of mind. Step out of the range of the television and any other distractions. Sometimes it helps if we imagine ourselves as one of these nonhuman guides, having chosen not to come down to Earth to learn, but instead in our wholeness and perfection have chosen to assist others from the lessons we ourselves have already been through. What would you want to do if you were one of those guides? You'd be dying to have a human in need ask you for your help so you could share your wisdom and creative ideas. At least, that is what I have thought. It helps me get over the feeling that I am bothering them, as if they have harp lessons they have to go to or something.

Find a place that is calm and comfortable. If you have a favorite room or spot in your house or apartment or garden, go there. Find your favorite cushion or chair to sit on, in other words, surround yourself with things you adore. The idea is that this will help you tune into the desired frequency.

I worked for several years with a young boy who had serious problems with rage and anger. During the beginning of our work, he showed considerable improvement, mostly because he was feeling better about himself on the inside. One time while working with him, I attempted to arm him with what I felt he needed every time he became overwhelmed with negative thoughts that then led to negative actions. I tried to get him to think of something or someone that always loved him. He answered that his mom and dad did. I asked him if he felt they always, no matter what, loved him and he always, no matter, what loved them. He said honestly, "No, sometimes I am mad at them or they are mad at me." "Okay, how about your little brother," I asked? "Yeah, well, no, not him either, even though I love him, sometimes he makes me really mad." I said to search his mind for something that was always there for him and always gave him a wonderful feeling every time he saw it. Just then his eyes got bright and he said, "My BUNNY!" His stuffed bunny was a gift to him as an infant and as long as he could remember, he had slept with it. My image was of the Velveteen Rabbit in the storybook. It probably had no more fuzz or eyes and a few missing body parts. Nonetheless, we had found what I was looking for, something that he could think about when he started feeling overwhelmed with negative feelings. He loved his bunny, no matter what, and felt his bunny loved him. This we prescribed as his bunny pill that he would take whenever and as often as he needed. That's what I am asking you to find.

When you begin connecting with your own personal guides, you're going to feel like you're sending a message off to an unknown recipient at an unknown address, uncertain that it will really make it. So in order to at least get the address right, tune the dial to nonphysical guides. To do this, what I have found that helps is trying to connect in an atmosphere of love. After you have successfully figured out how to connect, you can be in any mood and still receive and send effectively. Once after several years of connecting the soft way, I went to my spot and my favorite cushion and I demanded, "What the heck is going on here? I want answers and I want them now!" I was half afraid, still harboring childhood images of a vain God, that I was going to hear thunder and be told to be quiet and I would get my answers when they were dang well ready. But I didn't. What I heard was a very real answer to a very real question and it made a heck of a lot of sense. I said, "Now why didn't you tell me that before?" They said I never asked.

Which brings me to the next part. Asking. You don't have to phrase the question like you are an undeserving clod, or like you hang out with King James or even like you are ordering up a burger. It is about cooperation. Try to decide what is really bugging you. For example, if you are upset with something someone else has said or done to you, asking what is wrong with them really doesn't do you a whole lot of good. Maybe a question like, "Why was my reaction to what so and so did so violent, or why has it made me so sad?" What you will hear in your heart of hearts is a voice telling you about a deep fear that you really knew was there all along. This is particularly why so many people think that the voices are not from guides, because they already knew the answer somewhere inside. Where do you think these guides are getting their clues? You? We are not separate. Let me say that again. We are not separate. All of us access information about other people all the time just being around them, feeling their energy, vibrating with their stuff or just existing, whether in a body or not. Even death does not separate us.

When I first began trusting my own inner guidance or intuition, (they can be interchangeable since they come from the same source of infinite knowledge or organic wisdom), I had a few funny experiences. I worked at a company where part of my job was meeting with representatives from the company's many vendors. One day, I was talking to this nice man, really enjoying connecting with him, introducing him to our staff, all the while overwhelmed by the feelings of an infant coming from him. I tried to rationalize it by thinking he wore baby lotion or something like that. Then my brain piped in, he's really a little too old to have an infant of his own right now, but the feeling persisted so strongly that I gave in to my intuitive call and stopped him and asked, "Do you have a new child by any chance?" Oh my gosh, you'd think I had just blown apart the Aswan Dam! What a flood of pictures and laughing and delight and joy! It was incredible! He and his wife had been late in starting and were afraid they wouldn't conceive, and so on. WOW! That was the beginning of a very close relationship that lasted long after he left the company that brought him to ours. You may not hear the winning sweepstake numbers on your first phone call, but you will be gifted with treasures that enhance the human experience.

When asking, be honest and direct. Don't hedge your bet or try to make them think you're really not as vain as you are, remember, we are not separate, they know you already. We share the same fabric of our most inner beings. You can lay it out like, "I hurt. Why?" That's pretty direct. Try to stay away from things like, "Which will be best for me, option A or B?" Avoid this approach for two reasons, first, what is best? And secondly, what about option Q, something you haven't even thought of? What is best might be meeting a soul from a previous life to whom you owe money and you are ready to equal out that energetic debt now. So then when you make a decision based on what is best and it leads you to get ripped off of two grand (or repaying your karmic debt), you'll wonder why you ever listened to those stupid guides in the first place (don't try to sue me, I don't think you have a case!). Leave open-ended options if possible. Sometimes it requires letting your mind out of a box.

Many people say to me, there was no solution, so I didn't bother asking about that. In our limited minds there may be no obvious, acceptable solution, but there is always a door. That door may take you inside yourself, or into a contract you agreed upon before you can remember, or into facing your deepest fear, but there are always options. Sometimes when many things conspire against you, or you get fired from your job, a very real and wonderful thing happens, you stop doing something you hated, and what's left? Something you wanted to do, but your day job had gotten in the way.

Part of my old job entailed firing employees if I felt it was necessary. Of the few times I did, two of those employees are still my close friends. What I found was, when done in fairness and compassion, in other words, ego intact, they realized they hated the job they were doing or it wasn't suited for them anyway, and went on to do things they liked a whole lot better.

One of my closest friends asked me a few years ago, "How do you find that thing you were meant to do here on earth, in this lifetime?" I suggested looking at what makes you the happiest. He replied, "Nothing." He said he was an engineer and figured he always would be, but didn't really enjoy it all that much. I asked, "Well, what do you do, that when you do it, time passes really quickly?" "Oh," he said, "that's easy. That would be playing my guitar and writing songs. But I don't do it often, because I think it's taking me away from more constructive things." Within several weeks of making this personal discovery, the dot-com company he worked for went bankrupt. He was left without a job and instead of panicking, as he was fully prepared to do, he took the time between looking for work to play his guitar and write and record some of his own music. He felt awesome, and the better he felt, the more desirable he became, unlike the other unemployed engineers looking for work, and was offered another job fairly quickly. It was only part time at first. Maybe his soul was saying, "Hey, we're not giving this love up too fast. I'll help you pay rent if you let me out."

Pretty soon after that I got a call telling me that he'd joined a band in San Francisco and was loving it. He asked me to check out their web page where he was featured with the band. Not long after, he was sending me emails of the lyrics to his songs. I couldn't believe it. No wonder that was his calling. He was writing teen songs, with words that were powerful and honest, yet in their own language. It was filling a need, the universe accepted his unique offering and he was excelling! Once again, when logical direction eludes, ask your heart!

There is one more thing to be said about connecting with your guides, helpers and teachers on the nonphysical realm. They never ever chastise you. That means they don't belittle you, make fun of you or demean you in any way. If you hear voices doing that, they are coming from your own head. They are responding to negative beliefs about yourself. If you hear a voice that is responding in fear, it most likely is fear. If you want to be sure though, to determine if this is a warning trying to protect you from something, you simply ask, "Are you coming from fear?" Either the answer will repeat itself, not afraid to be confronted, or it will disintegrate. Most of the time when you get warning or safety type messages, they will not be accompanied by fear, you will just have a very strong sense of knowing that "I need to get out of here, NOW," or "I need to call my mother, NOW," or "I need to turn left, NOW," but it is neutral and direct. So when you feel overwhelmed with fear in relation to a question, try this trick, it's like shining a light on a dark thing. It's not dark anymore.

My idea about connecting with guides is that it makes being a human easier. What if you knew a very wise person who knew everything about everything or anything you could even think of and you never ever asked for their advice? That seems like a very unwise use of resources. Not only does it make life easier, but it makes it more fun. Everything you do becomes more fulfilling, from having relationships to completing a project. It adds an element of creativity, of surprise, of your highest possible solution, and it makes life less lonely too!

One beautiful winter day my husband and I decided to go up the mountain and go skiing. Normally, I love to ski and it is unusual that my warm-weather loving husband actually suggests it, but this one day every time I thought of myself skiing I felt weak. I didn't know what to make of it and kept making other suggestions, to perhaps take a hike instead. Finally, the time came to either go or not. I sat quietly in a room by myself and asked if skiing today would be beneficial for me. I got a very visual scene of myself with a left leg terribly distorted from an accident. Not sure if I planted that myself, or what the motivation would be, I tried another trick I use. I calmly found a neutral place, going skiing or not now didn't matter, and asked myself as an 80-year-old woman if I would regret going skiing today. She very plainly and loudly said, "Yes." I didn't go and will never know if it was intuition or something fabricated by my own wild imagination, but I didn't see any reason to find out.

Once you start having fun with your nonphysical companions, you will find that they place helpful things just where you are going to be, to assist you with more technical information than they can transmit or you could understand, like books, or resourceful people or healers or movies that contain a currently un-thought-of solution to a life puzzle. Some people call it synchronicity, but whatever you want to call it, it is connecting with the nonmaterial realm to assist in the material realm. And it is fabulous!

Several people a week ask me how they can know their guides. They believe they have them, they even suspect they have heard them. They ask if they have names, how many there are, and that sort of thing. I say, once again, ask. Years ago when I first started learning the energy healing work I now do, I was practicing with another student and after she identified something, I asked her how she knew that? She replied that she asked her guides and that if I wanted to know for myself, ask mine. I said, "Me? I have guides??" I thought that was for the very wise and swamied. She said, "Sure, I see three around you now." I didn't know whether to believe her or not, but knew she had been known to be psychic, and probed further. She said I should get to know them myself. I thought about it for months and one day woke up and knew that I was going to take the time to get to know these guides.

I went to a beautiful park overlooking the whole San Francisco Bay and began. "Let's start with you, I'll call you my Master Spirit Guide. Who are you? How can I know you?" I started with male/female as a gender that I could relate to. A name? A country that they most identified with while on Earth? It took some time. Some didn't want to be tied to a gender and others to a country, but I ended up with some way to identify each one from my human perspective.

Years later, a woman was working on my feet doing reflexology and she kept looking around me, up and over my shoulder. I finally asked her, "What are you looking at?" She said, "I have never seen such busy guides." She described them so I knew who was where and that she was right. I told her that I ask them to help me do my work and that I had asked them before I went to her place to begin to get my next client ready for our afternoon session. I was glad to know they weren't goofing off! It was a confirmation especially for me. Because even though I had worked with them for so long, I had never actually seen my guides, but had only felt their presence.

Recently, I became aware that your guides change as you change. When you begin something new, whether it is a hobby or a career, you may get a new guide. Sometimes they change, and other times you just get a new one for a while. Lately, as my life has been shifting from what I thought I was going to be doing forever, to what the Universe is reminding me I have yet to do, I felt devoid of my spirit guides for a while. I have never felt so lonely. I asked, " Where is everyone?" I only got the voice of a man, one I was not familiar with, saying that he was here doing some reconstruction, and my guides were being upgraded also. I started asking him loads of questions, like, "What the heck are you talking about and where is everyone and what are you doing and who sent you and what was wrong that I need this?" and so on. I heard the funniest little guy say, "Lady, I don't know nothin' 'bout any o' that, I'm just here fer rewirin'." I'm sure that was my own way of letting me know, this was a worker guy. This went on for a very lonesome and depressing month and then I suddenly felt like someone turned the light back on. Sitting in meditation I took a census around me, energetically, fully expecting my old familiar guides back. I then saw this smiling, joyful, redheaded woman, just beaming at me like we have known each other forever. "Who's the red head?"

I gather she is part of my new entourage and felt glad that she seemed so happy to be assigned to me. I am still not sure what she represents in my life, or what she is coming to help me with. Maybe she is my teacher-teacher, sent to assist me with my workshops and/or writing?

The point is, some guides (like your guardian angel) never ever change as long as your soul exists and others do. Think about Tchaikovsky, who was a lawyer until he was 40 and then became a concert pianist. He probably got a new set of guides with a completely different specialty. Then there are assistants you can call on, like a reference librarian, that everyone has access to, not as personal as your own team, but helpful when needed. I have found, the more you ask, the more there seems to be available. I have not yet reached a place where I find an end to resources, the more creatively you search, the more creativity is available.

IN SUMMARY

The human experience is a journey. You choose who goes with you and for how long. Getting the lessons, meeting the challenges, developing relationships of assistance and support (physical and nonphysical) certainly make the journey less painful, but there will always be times when we are challenged, when we don't understand and are in pain. Those times provide the opportunities for the greatest growth. Remember that the individuals who show up in our lives with a challenge represent a great gift. Don't forget you have tools to work with them. You have assistance and support. It may not feel like it, but look at all the tools just presented in this text. Maybe none will meet every need, but you will be guided to find what it is you personally need. Trust that you will.

In the words of Guatama Buddha:

> Do not believe in anything merely because it is said, nor in traditions because they have been handed down from antiquity, nor in rumors as such, nor in writings by sages because sages wrote them, nor in fancies that we may suspect to have been inspired in us by a deva, nor in inferences drawn from some haphazard assumption we may have made, nor in the mere authority of our teachers and masters. Believe when the writing, doctrine or saying is corroborated by your own consciousness.

Allow the physical, emotional, mental, egoic and soul bodies that make up you to participate in your energy existence, but keep the last word for the soul. It has access to Divine Organic Wisdom. It sees the bigger picture, it feels the existence of the Divine, and it is patient. If you haven't gotten anything else from this text, remember you are Divine, which means you know. Trust yourself to find the answers for you, allow yourself to claim your authentic self, not needing the authority of anyone or any organization, know the Divine resides in you. What are you not capable of, given free access to Divine Wisdom, Universal Power and Mother Nature's knowledge?

Appendix

NEGATIVE EMOTIONAL WORD LIST

Self-Blame	Failure
Self-Doubt	Rejected
Vulnerable	Overburdened
Paranoid	Aggravated
Feeling Stupid	Discomfort
Dislike of Self	Irritated
Self-Hate	Upset
Abandoned	Scapegoat
Isolated	Unjust
Separated	Betrayed
Loss of Support	Dishonored
Sense of Loss	Loss of Prestige
Powerless	Ill Health
Dominated	Overweight
Futility	Overworked
Apathy	Victim
Lazy	Castrated
Aimless	Frigid
Non-communication	Barren
Invaded	Poor
Confused	Arrogant
Concerned	Conceited
Nervous	Intolerant
Disillusioned	Judgmental
Dissatisfied	Ungrateful
Defensive	Dictatorial
Unappreciated	Overbearing
Misunderstood	Indignant

Repressed Aggression	Parental Disapproval
Sorry	Persecuted
Guilt	Trapped
Ashamed	Thwarted
Insincere	Judged
Violation of Integrity	Fanatic
Blasphemy	Obsessed
Cheated	Abhorrence
Disappointed	Hate
Embarrassed	Rivalry
Foolish	Malicious
Altercation	Fear
Conflict	Terror
Anger	Panic
Violence	Anguish
Rage	Torture
Mad	Cursed
Coveting	Unwanted
Jealousy	Unloved
Greedy	Unrequited Love
Resentment	Heartbroken
Hemmed In	Worthless
Used	Ugly
Indecisive	Grief
Insecure	Suicidal
Intimidated	Anxiety
Introverted	Heavyhearted
Inferior	Death
Inadequate	Hopeless
Naïve	Drab
Inability to Cope	Exhausted

POSITIVE EMOTIONAL WORD LIST

Connected	Free
Supported	Independent
Encouraged	Strong
Blessed	Fearless
Comforted	Passionate
Secure	Courageous
Abundant	Heroic
Bright	Innocent
Intelligent	Forgiven
Smart	Beautiful
Optimistic	Inviting
Magnetic	Kind
Confident	Peaceful
Centered	Calm
Directed	Balanced
Ambitious	Serene
Capable	Content
Focused	Relaxed
Grounded	Untroubled
Understood	Cherished
Helpful	Cared for
Merciful	Loved
Trusting	Accepted
Forthright	Adored
Healthy	Admirable

Happy
Joyful
Excited
Invigorated
Uplifted
Jovial
Energetic
Motivated

Worthwhile
Honored
Dignified
Praised
Appreciated
Valued

Thoughtful
Sensitive
Responsible
Compassionate

Sincere
Humble
Grateful
Genuine
Unique
Authentic
Honest
Gracious
Truthful

Adaptable
Clear
Mature
Intuitive
Open-minded
Wise
Aware
Unbiased

Purposeful
Organized
Successful
Masterful
Skillful
Industrious

Yielding
Cooperative
Flowing
Flexible

Loyal
Dependable
Encouraging
Loving

RESOURCES by the AUTHOR

WORKSHOPS
and
ENERGY HEALING SESSIONS

WORKSHOP

COMBINING SPIRIT AND CREATIVITY TO IMPROVE RELATIONSHIPS
with Julie Hutslar

How we understand and respond to our own relationships creates the fabric of our current lives, whether they are with parents, partners, or offspring; bosses, employees, coworkers, or clients. We often find ourselves repeating the same relationship patterns, hitting the same frustrating walls. Just as often we feel we are victims to other people's authority, manipulation or power over us. Or maybe we feel the by-products of someone's prejudice against us. What can we do?

In this unique workshop, Julie Hutslar offers new ways to view relationships, ways that change the dynamic altogether. See how the most challenging individuals in our lives are actually a soulful catalyst for much needed healing. This awareness beckons to us to reclaim our power, no longer feel out of control or victimized. Not only does she offer new understandings by looking at relationships through the spiritual lens, but she shares success stories of many of her clients. In addition, she introduces many methods to consciously change the way we deal with our challenging relationships, from learning how to speak to someone's higher self to extinguishing the male/female argument ritual.

She offers techniques in understanding key differences in how people communicate, identifying bases from which people operate, and how to create a safe haven to draw out the best someone has to offer. Ms. Hutslar herself creates a fun and unthreatening environment to help others open up to creative ideas for managing relationships (including the self), for entertaining new ideas on the purpose and energetics of relationships as well as suggestions for letting go of outdated, limiting beliefs that block the path to our highest self and ultimately our own healing and success.

This workshop is excellent for couples, people whose jobs include working with many personalities, those in human resources or sales, teachers, and people in management. It is a wonderful way to bring unity and teamwork to a group when the workshop is taken together either in a corporate environment or a work situation. Basically, anyone in a relationship can benefit from the new awarenesses and concepts of this workshop.

Julie synthesizes years of energy healing sessions, 20-some years as a practitioner of spiritual astrology, and even more practicing creative management in the workplace. Along with these she integrates the lessons of her own spiritual path swirled together by her intuition, creativity and awareness of lifetimes of relationships into her own personal, yet fascinating workshop guaranteed to stimulate change and spiritual growth.

For more information, to view her workshop schedule, or to host a workshop, contact Julie at **www.jrhutslar.com**

WORKSHOP

REMOVING UNCONSCIOUS BLOCKS TO HIGHER CREATIVITY
with Julie Hutslar

"Before you can be creative, you have to believe you're creative"

Many of us believe we are not creative, have been told we are not creative, and have even convinced ourselves we are not creative when all we have really done is unconsciously blocked the pathways to hear and receive our own unique creativity. These blockages can lead to low self-esteem, health disorders, difficulty solving problems, relationship issues and a general sense of unfulfillment.

These blocks may have been accumulated from school teachers who said the wrong thing to us at a vulnerable time, from parents who meant well, but didn't want to see us disappointed, or from ill-fated competitions or judgments. The results are individuals who keep their most prized possession, their unique creativity, bottled inside with no possible method of expression. Did you used to play the guitar, but haven't touched it in years? Did you think of yourself as an artist as a young child, but haven't picked up a pencil or brush in decades? Do you feel something trying to get out, but don't know how to communicate with this part of you? Do you feel fear whenever you are asked to do something creative, and so decline the offer?

Intuitive artist and energy healer, Julie Hutslar, combines her skills as a gifted watercolor artist with the tools of locating and removing blocks in our belief systems that keep us from knowing we are all born creative individuals. She draws upon many fun and adventurous methods and years of energy healing sessions to refind the creative voice. She utilizes the techniques of watercolor painting as a spontaneous way to begin letting that trapped creativity express its subconscious self. It has far reaching effects, way beyond painting, as it changes the way we see ourselves and our potential, from flower arranging, cooking, and musical ability to creative ways of solving business problems or relationship issues. It is about removing the negative images and thoughts we carry that sabotage our own success.

This workshop requires no previous experience in painting or even drawing. It is about opening creative channels and finding fulfilling ways to express oneself. It is for anyone who wants to unleash their own creative energy, for those who find themselves blocked but still sense there is more, for people who want to 'get back' that creativity they may have felt at one time in their life, or for those who are just ready to expand and are willing to believe there may be more for them.

The process takes place in a safe environment of positive feedback and sincere encouragement to allow the vulnerable creative part of you to come out and be nurtured and loved. So leave your internal critic at home and invest a few days in something that could change your life forever.

For more information, to view her workshop schedule, or to host a workshop, contact Julie at **www.jrhutslar.com**

INDIVIDUAL SESSIONS

ACCELERATED HEALING
with Julie Hutslar

One day you find yourself in a place where you feel there's an invisible ceiling keeping you from attaining what your mind says you can, what you believe you can, or what you feel you deserve, but there isn't really anyone or anything physically keeping you there. You then begin to realize the ceiling must have been somehow created within. You try being positive, but this nagging voice remains, holding you back. How do you change these beliefs if they are stored so inaccessibly inside?

Julie takes you on a journey through your own personal history to find the place and time where an incident occurred that allowed or prompted certain beliefs to be stored that are now limiting you. There she assists in turning the light off or depowering the belief, making it no longer part of the energy system that dictates your personal reality. As an example, if we believe subconsciously that we are *inferior*, then what we advertise (also unconsciously) is that we are less than others, getting passed over for a promotion, not valued by our partners, treated with disrespect by those who come into contact with us and not even treated with extravagance by ourselves. Everything from our relationships to the opportunities in career and finance that 'come our way' are experiences responding to our innermost beliefs. By embarking on this road to re-creating your reality, not only do you take ultimate responsibility for your own circumstances which stimulates a huge dose of empowerment, but you come to understand that you have helped create the existence you now call 'reality'.

Some of the changes that can occur as a result of removing these boundaries (endless as the individuals that seek this work) range from ending phobias, allowing limitless love into your life, to increasing the ability to reach mind-created goals: financial, emotional, physical or spiritual. The ceiling just isn't there anymore and nothing else has changed in your life except for some long-stored and hidden belief. Often a different understanding of an old and difficult relationship brings much needed light necessary for healing and spiritual evolution.

Essentially, your spirit is trying to grow from the experiences we have as humans, but unfortunately in the process, we misunderstand much of what is happening on a soul level, and interpret the situation through the lens of the ego. This creates lots of negative misinformation about ourselves and the world we live in. When we bump into these self-created boundaries again, we don't understand why they are there or where they came from. This is where Julie facilitates. She helps remove images of ourselves that dampen our self-esteem and ultimately keep us from being all we came here to be. How can we soar carrying 14 tons of personal garbage?

For more information or to discuss scheduling a session, contact Julie at **www.jrhutslar.com**

ABOUT THE AUTHOR

Julie Hutslar's life experiences have proven to be an excellent study for a book on relationships.

Creatively, she has been a professional artist most of her life, plays the piano and composes her own music, dances and sings with a freedom and abandon most of us only dream of, and is a gourmet chef. She lives in accord with the idea that, "When you are an artist, everything you do is art."

Academically, she has a Master's degree in International Relations from the Monterey Institute of International Studies.

Professionally in the business-world, her last position was a manager of a firm with over 70 employees and several offices. Her official title was Sales Manager, but her intangible place in the company might have been better titled "Relationships Manager." We've all known those who seem to always lend an empathetic ear to others in need, provide support both at work and beyond, and just hold the whole place together. At work, Julie was that person. Because of these extracurricular skills she was even interviewed for material for John Gray's excellent book on relationships in the office, *Mars and Venus in the Workplace*.

Professionally in the healing-world, she practices a method of energy, or spirit healing, she calls Accelerated Healing. In one-to-one client sessions she seeks to identify, reconcile, and remove belief patterns that negatively influence a person's life, preventing them from living the life they truly would love to live.

Julie speaks several languages. She has lived from Hawaii to Florida to Europe and many places in between, gaining new experiences from the people she meets. She is comfortable with people of all levels of society; rich or poor, old or young, of any nationality or gender, and as a testament to her accepting energy, animals and children take to her immediately.

Julie is living life artistically and creatively. Hopelessly positively poled (see chapter 3), she is creating her own existence, a goal she hopes to share with the rest of us through her writing, seminars, and healing sessions.